Wakefield Press

SERVANTS • DEPOTS •

in colonial South Australia

Marie Steiner was born in Port Augusta, South Australia, and grew up in the state's south-east. She studied history and tutored at the University of Adelaide, and lectured in history at a teachers' college. After changing disciplines, Marie worked as a consultant to women's shelters and in a variety of social administration positions. She now lives in Adelaide.

SERVANTS • DEPOTS •

in colonial South Australia

Marie Steiner

Wakefield Press

Wakefield Press
16 Rose Street
Mile End
South Australia 5031
www.wakefieldpress.com.au

First published 2009
This edition published 2018
Reprinted 2019

Cover designed by Lahn Stafford Design
Typeset by Wakefield Press

ISBN 978 1 74305 578 6

A catalogue record for this book is available from the National Library of Australia

Wakefield Press thanks Coriole Vineyards for continued support

CONTENTS

Acknowledgements

I am very grateful to my friend, Janet Callen, who has written about the wreck of the *Nashwauk* off Harriott's Creek, near Moana, in 1855. She compiled all the available information about those named on the *Nashwauk* passenger list. Curiosity about the fortunes of the rescued single Irish female passengers led me to investigate the servants depots which were subsequently established throughout the colony to accommodate them and others arriving throughout the year.

For those readers interested in exploring family connections with servant girls placed in any of the depots, names have been provided whenever possible and references supplied. Newspapers of the time were used extensively. Local history groups and regional National Trust bodies provided considerable help, as did staff from the Catholic Archives, the Family History Centre at the Marion Church of Jesus Christ of the Latter Day Saints and the Genealogy Society at Unley. Those descendants of the *Nashwauk* passengers who could be identified and contacted readily made available retrieved family histories. This information proved invaluable.

Government bodies have, without exception, been helpful, particularly the archivists at State Records.

Preface

The year 1855 saw 'excessive female immigration' in the colony of South Australia. Far more ships bringing assisted migrants arrived at Port Adelaide than ever before with a disproportionate number of single females coming to be servants. At the same time the depressed harvest of the previous year resulted in settlers being unable to afford domestic labour. The efforts of the Colonial Government to deal with this increase in the number of unwanted single females throughout the year was innovative and at times caused unrest and even scandal. The consequent establishment of servants depots and their management by a Female Immigration Board (FIB) reveals much about the paternalism, social and industrial attitudes, and particularly the condition of women, at that time.

This is the history of the servants depots, distributed throughout the settled areas to provide care and work situations for unemployed single women. The country depots were temporary establishments, each lasting for about six months. Special attention is given to those young Irish girls who were passengers on the *Nashwauk*, a ship that was wrecked in May 1855 at Harriott's Creek, Moana, with no loss of life. The *Nashwauk* is one of only ten ships listed under the *Historic Shipwrecks Act 1981* and its anchor is on display at the Moana Caravan Park. Many of these single females were placed, from a depot, as servants in country areas, particularly in the Clare District. Their stories are typical of the experiences of their compatriots throughout the colony and reveal a little of what it was like to be an unattached woman in mid-nineteenth-century South Australia.

CHAPTER ONE

The Background: Female Immigration in 1855–1856

Ellen Moore, a twenty-year-old domestic servant from Kings in Ireland, was one of the single female passengers who arrived at Port Adelaide by steamer from the wreck of the *Nashwauk* in May 1855, after three months at sea. Immigrants were allowed to spend fourteen days on board ship whilst accommodation and employment were arranged, and so those from the wreck were comfortably accommodated in an empty iron store for two weeks.

During this time Ellen would have seen the Customs House, as well as a clutter of warehouses and shipping offices. Then, in the company of some of her fellow passengers, she was taken by bullock dray along the rough track to town. With her she took her mattress, blankets, cup, plate and cutlery from the ship. There was a horse-drawn two-wheeled cart, the 'port cart'; available, but only for fee-paying customers. Ellen would have lumbered past Crawford's Brewery, the solid stone Adelaide Gaol, Trinity Church, a quarry, an iron foundry, Government House (set well back from the road), and some brick houses as well as dilapidated wooden tenements.

Her initial impressions of the town must have been very confusing. At this time the streets of Adelaide were undrained, unpaved and fetid. Behind the cottages at the west end of town there were open cesspools, dung heaps, butcher's offal and crowded piggeries. Water was still being delivered by cart from the River Torrens, but there were impressive new buildings along King William Street: the Supreme Court House, the Treasury Building, and the General Post Office had all recently been completed. Hindley Street was already a busy retail centre, with shops selling shawls, ribbons, laces, china, glass and other domestic necessities with which she would be familiar and there was another grocery store (Hutchins) in Gouger Street.

Ellen was surprised and presumably somewhat shocked to find that she was taken to temporary accommodation in the German Hospital, completed in 1852 but still unoccupied in Carrington Street until extensions were finished at the Female Immigration Depot (FID). Whatever had been arranged for her future? What was the colony providing?

The girls, like Ellen, who arrived on the *Nashwauk* had left home and crossed half the world in the hope of finding employment and husbands. They were a small component of a much larger group of mainly domestic servants, most of them Irish, who came in 1855. They were all assisted migrants and the responsibility not only of the Colonial Government but also of the British Government which had recruited and selected them. An outline of the interactions between both authorities provides a background to the decisions made by the Colonial Government of South Australia which so directly impacted on their lives.

The colony's Immigration Agent was responsible for the reception of all immigrants on arrival, ensuring they had been properly treated on board ship. It was also his duty to assist with their accommodation and employment. Dr Handasyde Duncan, a Scotsman with a medical degree from Glasgow University, registered as a surgeon and physician in both Glasgow and Edinburgh, had been the Immigration Agent for some years. He had come to Adelaide in 1840 and was a well-established colonist. In his quarterly reports, he made recommendations to the Governor on the labour needs of the colony, and these were relayed to the Secretary of State in Britain, responsible for the Colonial Office. The Colonial Land and Emigration Commission (CLEC), housed in London, was the body responsible for the survey and sale of lands and the emigration of labourers to each of the Australian colonies. During the year 1855, due to political manoeuvres in the British Parliament, there were no less than four appointments to the position of Secretary of State, but the administration remained consistent as Herman Merivale, previously Professor of Political Economy at Oxford University, remained permanent head of the Colonial Office from 1847–1859. Nevertheless there was a problem matching the demand and supply of labour in South Australia. The turnaround time for correspondence between London and the colony was, in the days of sail, about eight months. A year might elapse before the colonial demands were met and those migrants with the required skills arrived.

Demand for farm labourers was strong in mid 1854, but had almost evaporated early in 1855, owing partly to a very poor harvest. The colony's Acting Governor, Boyle Travers Finniss, sent the Immigration Agent's March quarterly report to London in May. Dr Duncan emphasised the disparity between the number of young women sent out from Ireland, the depressed harvest of 1854 and the consequent wish by colonists to reduce their establishment. At that time 138 female immigrants were being supported by government; 126 were Irish. Duncan wrote that employers preferred Scottish and English girls as they were better trained for domestic service.[1] In his next quarterly report, he wrote:

> In ordinary seasons and circumstances the gradual and well timed introduction of cheap hand labour in an agricultural country such as this would be beneficial, but these young women have been sent in such numbers as to be at any time in excess of the numbers to find employment, and in the present

> season and after the failure of last year's harvest, they have arrived at a time when the price of all kinds of food is so high that their labour would not be an equivalent for their actual consumption of provision.[2]

Of the girls who arrived on the *Nashwauk* almost forty were registered on the passenger list as either farm labourers or dairymaids.

Accommodation for the increasing number of unemployed females was becoming a major problem. Matthew Mooorhouse was the Comptroller of the Destitute Asylum, located east of Government House on parklands north of North Terrace. He was responsible for providing care for the female assisted migrants at the FID next to the Destitute Asylum, and had to use temporary facilities (including the German Hospital where Ellen was placed) in June and July whilst the depot was being expanded. It was this lack of accommodation which provoked action by the new Governor of South Australia who arrived in June 1855, replacing B.T. Finniss who had acted as Governor since Sir Henry Young had left in December 1854.[3]

Richard Graves MacDonnell was born in Dublin in 1814, a son of the provost of Trinity College. He studied law, was called to the Irish bar in 1838 and then practised in London. He had been Chief Justice of Gambia and Governor or Administrator of several British settlements prior to his appointment to South Australia. Not long after his arrival he dissolved the Legislative Council and issued writs for new elections, so that a new Constitution Bill could be considered and a form of self-government established. According to one historian in 1876, MacDonnell was 'exceedingly popular during the whole of his administration'.[4] Another wrote, 'He possessed considerable ability and energy of character, which, added to a pleasant and genial manner, made him exceedingly popular'.[5]

His response to the unanticipated expense of maintaining an

increasing number of unemployed women was immediate. Towards the end of June, very soon after he had arrived in the colony, MacDonnell wrote to Sir John Russell, Acting Principal Secretary of State, responsible for the CLEC. He reported there were currently 203 girls accommodated temporarily at the newly built but vacant German Hospital. Having conversed freely with them, he was greatly surprised that two-thirds should have been selected at all, ignorant as they were of the duties of a domestic servant. He noted that there was great prejudice against them, just now, because of the class of person sent out by the emigration commissioners. MacDonnell was about to apply to all district councils and stipendiary magistrates requesting information about the demand for domestic or farm servants in each area and suggesting the establishment of depots for female immigrants. He was not optimistic because it was the season when agricultural labour was in least demand. When, and if employed on a seasonal basis, the girls would be left to find their way back to the 'Asylum for the Destitute where they must either be received or be driven forth to a disreputable course of life'. There would be considerable expense involved in establishing country depots but 'Her Majesty's Government, however, will probably agree with me, that expense must now be a secondary consideration'. He asked that all emigration of single females not accompanied by a near relative be stopped immediately.[6] This letter, of course, did not arrive in London for several months.

The idea of establishing depots, distributed throughout the colony, and administered by district councils, was not MacDonnell's. A letter to the editor of the *South Australian Register* dated 19 May, written by a 'District Councillor of the South' noted that the already large number of unemployed healthy female immigrants had increased after the wreck of 'that ill-fated vessel the *Nashwauk*'. He felt these girls were 'not very likely to get employment in the neighbourhood of

Adelaide' and they were more suitable to the general occupation of country life than those who had been brought up in a town. They could be distributed throughout the colony. He suggested the government send four or five to each district council and guarantee the expense of their support until engaged. 'I feel convinced that in three weeks every girl would find a situation.'

No doubt this idea was widely discussed during the next few weeks. At the end of June, MacDonnell sent a letter through his Colonial Secretary to district councils, magistrates, clergy and justices of the peace. He stated that there were several hundred single females – immigrants from Ireland – for whom there was no work.

> Many ... are highly respectable, and well qualified as in-door domestic servants; but the majority of them have not yet acquired experience sufficient to render them immediately useful in that capacity. They are, however, strong healthy and willing to be employed as farm servants, having most of them, already served in that capacity.

MacDonnell asked for an assessment of the advantages of establishing servants depotss, the possible cost of establishing the necessary facilities and the availability of housing.[7]

The response was generally supportive. The Roman Catholic Bishop, twenty magistrates and fourteen district council chairmen approved.[8] Those councils unable to set up depots nevertheless made enquiries in their areas. C. Hewitt, Chairman of the District Council of Yankalilla and Myponga, reported that by 2 July 1855 fifteen positions had been found, and listed the names of the settlers and the positions each required.[9] The three settlers from Myponga were quite specific in their requirements. One servant was to be able to milk, another was to be a nursemaid and the other a general servant.

Unfortunately a note on the front of this memo from Hewitt to the Colonial Secretary indicated that it was not received until 30 July. 'This letter has been very long delayed apparently.' It was not until August that sixteen girls were taken on board the *Yatala* to Yankalilla. Very probably another servant had been requested in the intervening period. The Select Committee – appointed by the Legislative Council early in 1856 to report on female immigration – provided figures indicated that seventeen had been sent to Yankalilla from the Central Depot (another name for the Adelaide FID) by 28 January 1856.

Some suggestions made by the magistrates were highly imaginative. One thought the government should offer a bounty to those settlers who provided employment and another that the government should cover the cost of wages for the first six months. One recommended the establishment of a washhouse and laundry in Adelaide; another the cultivation of mulberry trees for silkworms so employment could be provided.[10]

There were some objections to the employment of Catholics, and to the poor quality of Irish servants. A total of ten magistrates and eight district council chairmen were opposed to the establishment of depots.[11] Various suggestions were made to alleviate the problem. Four magistrates suggested that the immigrants should be shipped back to England! Three suggested that female immigration be stopped.

Early in July MacDonnell toured the colony, using the mail run, to meet with councillors from potential depot areas. He went on horseback in the company of the Surveyor General, the Harbourmaster and two others, firstly to Willunga, then to Myponga, Yankalilla, Normanville and Port Elliot. He proceeded, by railway, to Goolwa, and then by boat to the Murray. He visited Wellington, Moorundie, Truro, Willaston and Gawler, 'selecting there a house for the reception of about 30 Irish Female Immigrants'.[12] He had travelled 500 miles in eight-and-half days.

On 21 August MacDonnell wrote to Sir John Russell[13] forwarding Dr Duncan's immigration report for the quarter ending 30 June. It showed that fifteen ships had arrived with 4464 souls.

> The single women who arrived during the quarter were in gross number 1446: of these, 1016 were sent from Ireland. In the Report for the quarter ended March 31, 1854, and in every Quarterly Report since that time, it has been stated that the young women sent here were generally of a class quite unsuited to the wants of the Colonists – accustomed to out-door farm work, they are quite unfit for domestic services.[14]

The Governor spoke of abuses in the system by which immigrants receive their embarkation orders.

> Nearly one fifth of those arriving here have applied for other States. Out of 564 Irish female immigrants rationed by Government only 286 had applied to be sent here. [72 had applied for Sydney, 159 for Melbourne, 3 for Geelong, 1 for America, and 43 were doubtful.] Many of the remainder had been induced to come because they had been informed by the agents of the Commissioners that they could reach the other colonies from Adelaide.[15]

Duncan, in his report, said:

> As we have nothing but the assertion of many of those persons before us, it is impossible to know, certainly, whether they are really true; but, in confirmation of these statements, some of them have given me the addresses, in the other Colonies, of their relatives to whom they wished to be sent. I must confess that I attach some credit to a statement so corroborated.

In the classified return of Irish female immigrants supported by government in the German Hospital at 27 June, provided by Comptroller of the Destitute Poor Establishment, Matthew Moorhouse,[16] many of the girls from the *Nashwauk* were listed as having applied for either Melbourne or Sydney. Ellen Moore said she had applied for Melbourne. Another, twenty-year-old Margaret Moore, also from Kings so presumably either a twin or a cousin, had applied for Sydney. It is not possible to ascertain which city was the originally intended destination for each girl. After a period of trauma involving shipwreck, displacement, crowded emergency accommodation and bleak employment prospects, it is not surprising that so many claimed to have applied to be sent elsewhere.

There is some evidence that at least two *Nashwauk* passengers who were not recorded as staying at the German Hospital had applied for other destinations prior to embarkation at Liverpool. Anastasia Collins or Cullen, a twenty-five-year-old from County Kilkenny, later told a Select Committee that she had applied for passage to Melbourne. Her parents had been dissatisfied when she got her sailing order for Adelaide but were told by the 'person they paid the money to' that it would be quite easy to get from Adelaide to Melbourne. She had a friend in Melbourne, and none on board the *Nashwauk*.

Another witness, Mary Riley, from Cork, is very difficult to identify. Her name is recorded as Byall in a table in the minutes of evidence, but there is neither a Mary Riley nor a Mary Byall recorded on the *Nashwauk* passenger list – or in the German Hospital. A letter from the Emigration Office in London written in August 1856 refers to a Mary Riley (Ready?) who was a *Nashwauk* passenger. However, Mary Ready (possibly confused with another named Ready) came from Limerick not Cork, and was very probably the Mary Reedy who stayed at the German Hospital! Whatever her name, this witness called Mary Riley had a very demoralising story. In Cork she had never been engaged in service and had always lived with her parents. She had applied for Sydney, where she had cousins 'doing well', but was told there was no vessel sailing for Sydney and the *Nashwauk* did not have enough passengers. At home she had milked, washed and done housework. (She was ill for five months after arrival, had never been sent to a country depot, had no friends in the colony and had been nine months in the depot.) She had no offers of employment and no reply to her letters to Sydney.[17]

Twelve girls from the *Nashwauk* were listed as having left Adelaide for Melbourne and Sydney by February 1856, in an appendix to the minutes of evidence in the Select Committee's report. They all had money and a letter confirming that they had contacts interstate. The issue of emigrants applying for other states on their embarkation papers remained contentious for some time. The *Government Gazette* quoted a letter from the Emigration Office in London to MacDonnell, dated 19 August 1856, repudiating claims made in a report in the *Adelaide Observer* that a number of females had been sent to Adelaide against their will.

> The number of young women alluded to (whose names are given in the accompanying Schedule) was twenty. Of these, the first eighteen applied from the first to be sent to SA; and never as far as we can find, intimated any wish to be sent elsewhere. The nineteenth, M.A. O'Brien, applied, in the first instance, to be sent to New South Wales but afterwards requested that her destination might be altered to Adelaide, that she might accompany Mary Munane; and she was accordingly transferred to an Adelaide ship.
>
> There remains only one person, Anastasia Cullen, who applied for a passage to Victoria, but was eventually sent to Adelaide. We cannot trace in this office the reason for the change; but we have applied for further information ...[18]

The names on the schedule sent from London confirmed that the two girls from the *Nashwauk* were M. Riley (Byall?) and A. Cullen (Collins?).

Governor MacDonnell also discussed the use of false names. Comptroller Moorhouse had explained that once girls had got their embarkation papers, parents often would not let them go, and so sold their papers for five shillings. One female had consequently acquired a passage even though she came directly from a penitentiary! There is no evidence that any of the *Nashwauk* passengers were using false names.

The letter the Governor sent to Russell dated 24 September indicated he was very angry.[19] His letter sent in June had probably not yet arrived in London. MacDonnell said that of the 8600 immigrants who had arrived this year before 1 September, 2800 were single women, and 2047 of these were from Ireland. He quoted the Immigration Agent's comments in his quarterly report that the colony had the 'greatest difficulty in finding employment for the class of young women who were sent here'. Nevertheless the CLEC had increased the numbers and more than 1000 women had been sent out in just one quarter. MacDonnell quoted the March 1855 census which indicated that the total population (excluding 'Natives' and the military) in South Australia was 85,821. (The *BLUE BOOK OF SOUTH AUSTRALIA*, a statistical report produced by the Colonial Secretary's Office recorded 97,387.) There was no category for farm servants in this census, perhaps a reflection of the difficulty the colony's small land-holders experienced enticing labour to isolated areas.

In his address to the first session of the newly appointed Legislative Council on 2 November 1855, Governor MacDonnell said that despite the depression caused by the deficient harvest of the last year, scarcely any able-bodied immigrants remained on the hands of the government, except the females from Ireland. He was very concerned that nearly 800 were lodged and rationed either in rural depots or in town.[20]

Nevertheless his complaints were being acknowledged. In response to his June letter, a reply, dated 10 October, from the Emigration Office in London stated: 'we took immediate steps to discontinue the emigration to South Australia of Irish single women unaccompanied by their parents.' Reference was made to a New South Wales report that indicated the number of emigrants from Ireland, Scotland and Wales were chosen in proportion to the United Kingdom's population distribution. However, 'as we were aware that the original founders of the colony of South Australia were English and Scottish we endeavoured to keep down the Irish proportion'. Figures were quoted for 1847–1852 indicating that the Irish proportion was only fifteen percent. The commissioners explained their current difficulties in recruiting emigrants, claiming that as English domestic servants were well paid and cared for, the colony did not attract them, and they 'can't be got to emigrate'. Women of 'unimpeachable character' had been selected until 1852. This letter did not arrive in Adelaide until late January 1856.[21]

A few days later MacDonnell addressed another scathing letter to the Secretary of State, Earl Grey: MacDonnell saw

> no reason for sending here, suddenly in one year, from Ireland, not merely more than half of the entire Female Immigrants, but nearly treble the number of the United English and Scottish Immigrants.

He requested that all assisted immigration be discontinued until further notice.[22] In the *Register* dated 12 February 1856, MacDonnell published his letter requesting the cessation of all immigration, and the text of the reply he had received from the Emigration Office in London to his earlier letter.

By 20 February there were 345 single Irish female emigrants rationed by the government in the various depots. There were none from England or Scotland.[23] Three ships arriving in February brought a total of only 129 female immigrants. Another six were admitted from on board a ship arriving in March.[24] Figures vary, inevitably. According to the daily *Register*[25], the *Navarino* had arrived in February bringing forty-two domestic servants, while the *South Australian Government Gazette* records only 35. Whichever way, the figures indicate that MacDonnell's correspondence with the CLEC was having the desired effect. The number of female domestic and farm servants being sent to the colony had been drastically reduced.

On 25 January 1856, a proposal was made in the Legislative Council

> That a Select Committee be appointed to inquire into the circumstances which led to the introduction of three thousand and upwards of Single Female Immigrants; their position in this Colony, and the expense attending their support and distribution; and the manner in which rations have been issued to persons out of employment; with power to call for papers, persons, and reports.

A Select Committee of five was duly appointed and required to report on Friday 15 February – an amazingly short time by today's standards. The committee examined documents, took evidence from the Immigration Agent and the officers in charge of the Female Immigrant Depot, questioned immigrants, 'and sought additional information from ... experienced colonists recently sojourning in Europe'.

The committee reported that a total of 11,871 assisted migrants arrived in South Australia in 1855; 4049 were single adult females. Nine more government ships arrived at Port Adelaide than in the previous year.[26] Tables listed the number of unemployed single female emigrants rationed by government from May to January 1856.[27]

Figures from different sources varied, of course, depending on definitions and the method of collation. Classifications, as well, varied constantly, influenced by employment prospects at any particular time. Whilst not statistically reliable, figures can nevertheless give an overall indication of the type of immigrant arriving. One historian provides a table which illustrates that in 1855 there arrived a total of 2456 domestic servants and 337 farm labourers, 48 dairymaids, 11 cooks, 15 seamstresses and 19 laundry maids.[28] On the *Nashwauk* passenger list, well over half of the total of 258 were classified as single women. Only five were not Irish. At that time girls aged fourteen and over were considered adults and those who were members of a family group were included in this classification of single women.

What then happened to Ellen Moore and her compatriots? How successful were they in finding work in a very restricted market, in which they were competing with an ever-increasing influx of new arrivals throughout the year? Where were they accommodated? How many were sent to one of the newly established servants depots in the country?

Each depot had its own tumult: there was a scandalous fracas at the Adelaide Depot; there were initially no mattresses at Gawler where straw was used for bedding; police were called in to the Willunga Depot; an overturned cart resulted in a tragic death at the Mount Barker Depot; and a young girl was expelled for insubordination from the Robe Depot; the Clare Matron was threatened with dismissal; girls 'entirely unfit' for country service were sent to the Encounter Bay Depot; and there were claims of misconduct at Kapunda, the last depot to be established.

Ellen Moore and other *Nashwauk* passengers were the very first residents of the empty hospital building located in the city's south-eastern corner near where St John's Church stands today. It had been initially rented for eight weeks while extensions were made to the Adelaide Immigration Depot. The *Adelaide Observer* of 19 May 1855 reported that the premises 'afforded very extensive and excellent accommodation'. However, by the end of June, as more immigrants flowed in from other ships, the hospital accommodation originally intended for 180 became quite inadequate. Maintaining clean facilities was very difficult and overcrowding presented health risks. Fortunately for Ellen, she was transferred directly to the Clare Depot towards the end of July. The hospital building was vacated by August when all remaining single female servant girls were moved to the Adelaide Depot.

CHAPTER TWO

The Adelaide Female Immigration Depot

The Immigration Agent, as well as being responsible for visiting each incoming ship and assisting immigrants, worked with the Destitute Board in providing relief and assistance to those in need. Facilities for female immigrants were thus linked with the provision of facilities for the destitute – the disabled, chronically ill, those convalescing from hospitalisation, pregnant and abandoned women, deserted and widowed families. By 1850, the colony's Destitute Board, which had been established the previous year, was finding the huts it used in Emigration Square, west of the corner of North and West terraces, were not providing sufficient accommodation for those requiring indoor relief. The military barracks, the first cottages to be built on the parklands between North Terrace and the River Torrens, were rented as a temporary measure while the Colonial Architect prepared plans for a Destitute Asylum. This was built in 1853, and enlarged the next year with another room and then a shed for boxes. Today the approximate location is that of the Migration Museum complex on Kintore Avenue.

The Female Immigration Depot (FID) comprised assorted buildings which had been accumulated over a few years. It was described in early March in the *Register*:

> Adjoining the Destitute Asylum to the northwards (currently the site of the University of Adelaide) is the depot for newly

> arrived female emigrants – a substantial, though insufficient building, well walled in. There is at present only one dormitory which could not hold more than sixty beds.

There was a small mess room which served as a kitchen, a 'convenient washing shed', two store rooms and a shed for boxes, 'not nearly large enough'. The Matron had the two front rooms facing the river and there was a little office.[1] The drains were repaired in April. New buildings to accommodate 400 women began in June and took two months to complete. During this time new arrivals were placed either in the unused German Hospital or in the armoury of the Police Barracks, until the new Depot was finished by the end of August.[2] These facilities must have looked very uninviting. In July, a journalist for the *Adelaide Times*, a daily newspaper, described the blank look of despair on the faces of the '140 young women who were yesterday brought up from the Port' often ending in 'a bursting flood of tears'.[3]

The approach to the armoury was gravelled, window sashes eased, a mesh shed erected,[4] extra ventilation provided, and a water closet constructed.[5] There was a request for bunks from Comptroller Matthew Moorhouse to the Colonial Secretary Finniss in August, as the girls were moving from the armoury[6] and the bunks which had been fitted as temporary bedding for the immigrants were to remain as fixtures.[7]

The provision of food in the depot appears to have been adequate. A memo from Finniss to Moorhouse on 2 July 1855 outlined the rations which were to be issued at the depot, similar to those at the Destitute Asylum: 20 oz of bread, 8 oz of meat, 2 oz of sugar, ½ oz of tea were provided daily for each adult. The bread, at both establishments, was to be of second quality, except that issued to children (those under fourteen years of age).[8] The Auditor General had suggested to the Destitute Board that brown rather than white bread be issued.[9]

However brown bread was stopped in July.

> The Destitute Asylum is at present used as much for a hospital as for anything else and for patients with relaxed bowels the brown bread would be very unsuitable.[10]

In early September, Governor MacDonnell allowed Moorhouse to purchase 500 pairs of boots and some other articles of dress 'to prepare these young women for domestic service' – as some girls had been in the depot for four to six months.[11] Already 200 pairs had been given out and the knowledge that the government was supplying boots

> has spread far and wide. Many have left their situations to enter the Depot and procure boots. It is a nice point to issue what is necessary and at the same time not to render the Depot sufficiently attractive to induce them to come into it.[12]

Even in the early twentieth century it was customary, in Scotland and Ireland, for young women to be barefooted, except in winter, so the incentive of free boots must have been very attractive, as Moorhouse observed.

Moorhouse reported on 21 September 1855 that there were 720 girls in the FID and 180 more at the Port. There were eight ward matrons, each paid five shillings per week, and two cooks paid seven shillings a week, to deal with this large number. The main problem was insufficient space. With great detail and with specific measurements about cubic space Moorhouse illustrated that more accommodation was necessary. Although well ventilated, the rooms were not meant to hold more than ninety adults, each having a space of ten square feet.[13] By the end of September, 'for the health and cleanliness of the girls whilst at the depot',[14] £6,000 had been approved for building additions to the Destitute Asylum and the FID.[15]

Approval for the erection of a 'foul ward' was given in October[16] to provide segregation for those with venereal diseases. It was agreed that the Colonial Surgeon was to come twice a day.[17] In the same month clothes rails and pegs were put in and two more openings for ventilation were made for the new Ward Six.[18]

There can be no doubt that the Colonial Government continuously upgraded facilities in the Adelaide Depot in an attempt to provide adequately for the influx of residents. Ellen Moore would have certainly been as physically comfortable as at home if she had been moved there from the German Hospital.

CHAPTER THREE

Assault at the Adelaide Depot

A 'disturbance' at the Adelaide Depot in September 1855 exemplified the impact of excessive female immigration on the limited resources of the colony, on the people trying to deal with the problem, and on the girls themselves. Governor MacDonnell immediately ordered the Destitute Board, chaired by Father Michael Ryan, to hold an inquiry into the alleged assault on a servant girl by Comptroller Matthew Moorhouse.

Each ward at the depot was calculated to hold ninety girls. Moorhouse customarily tried to rotate bed positions and distribute newcomers amongst various wards where there were vacancies. On Saturday, 8 September 1855, a general order was issued for all corner occupants to move to the centre of their wards in anticipation of fifty-three new arrivals from the Port. The girls arrived at 4 o'clock and Mr Walker, the Ward Clerk, allocated seven to Ward Four which had only seventy-five occupants. Margaret Fay, who had been Sub-Matron on the ship in which she had travelled to Adelaide, refused to move. She and another witness, Ann Mulvaney, said that they had been in a corner position for three months. At the inquiry, Margaret said she had not been present when the general order was issued. She did not see why she should leave the corner and asked Moorhouse, when he had come to investigate reports of disobedience, if she was being told to move because she was Irish and the newcomers were English. In fact, only two of the seven new girls allocated to the ward were English. Moorhouse, having ascertained this, asked Fay and Mulvaney to leave, but still Margaret Fay refused to move. From the accumulation of evidence given to the inquiry, by the Ward Matron Mrs Mealy and others, the subsequent events can be reconstructed. Moorhouse had taken Margaret Fay by the shoulder and the left breast, drew her from her box in the corner and pitched her forward with force onto the floor. She had got up and returned to her box. In response, Moorhouse called in two police constables to take her to the Destitute Asylum. However other girls rescued her and he had to call in four more policemen. Again the girls surrounded her so that she could not be found. Although there are no surviving records, it is very probable that the recalcitrant Margaret Fay was not permitted to remain in the servants depot.

The *Adelaide Times* ensured the event became very public. On Monday 10 September there was a report that three distressed female immigrants had come to the paper's office on Saturday evening to tell of the incident, at the same time that Dr Woodforde, a magistrate, was calling in for his paper. He agreed to go and check the facts. The details were relayed with relish. The public was outraged, claimed the journalist, using inflammatory inaccuracies. The girls were called 'defenceless orphans', and there was a reference to fourteen policemen with sticks and staves and girls throwing stones!

In response, the Governor consulted with members of the Executive Council as to whether or not the investigation should be public. The majority felt it important the government be seen desirous of punishing any party guilty of misconduct, and so the Colonial Secretary, B.T. Finniss, wrote to the Chairman of the Destitute Board.

> His Excellency is of the opinion that no objection should be made to the admission of any reporter for the Public Press

> who may desire to be present at the investigation to be held this afternoon by the Board, of the circumstances connected with the recent disturbance in the FID [Female Immigration Depot].[1]

Moorhouse had been a member of the board for some years in his role as Protector of Aborigines. After his appointment as Comptroller of the Destitute Poor in January 1855 he assumed responsibility for keeping minutes of all board meetings and for signing all correspondence. The findings of the inquiry, therefore, caused little surprise, although there could be no doubt that he had physically thrown a servant girl across the floor.

> The Board find that M. Fay thrice refused to move from the place she and others occupied in Ward 4; that on the impulse of the moment and without intending to do her any harm, Mr Moorhouse laid hold upon her and as some witnesses testify, threw her upon the ground.[2]

The board decided that no legal or judicial intervention was appropriate as the matters were so 'trivial'.

'The Late Fracas at the Immigration Depot' read a headline in the *Register*, had similarly reported the case on Thursday, 13 September, with the same headlines, commenting that the board had first resolved to hold the inquiry behind closed doors, but after lengthy discussion had agreed to admit reporters.

The decision made by the board of inquiry was unanimously criticised by all three newspapers. The editor of the *Adelaide Times* was adamant: 'Neither Mr Moorhouse's position as Magistrate nor his Superintendency of the Depot invests him with the right of having recourse personally to physical force.'[3] These matters were certainly not trivial, according to the popular press.

Governor MacDonnell wrote:

> The whole affair is injuring the immigrants very much because people are deterred from seeking servants from an asylum in which so much notoriety is unavoidable.

MacDonnell's concern was the publicity given to this exhibition of 'very great insubordination'.[4]

The most significant consequence of the disturbance in the Central Depot was the establishment of the Female Immigration Board (FIB).

CHAPTER FOUR

The Female Immigration Board

Not long after this much-publicised disturbance, Matthew Moorhouse, as Superintendent, wrote to Colonial Secretary Finniss recommending the establishment of a board to help him manage all the female immigration depots. Further to this, on 24 September 1855 Moorhouse provided a list of country depots, their distance from Adelaide in miles, the number of immigrants sent, numbers hired, and the probable number remaining. He listed Penola and Mount Gambier with a note indicating that these areas had been supplied from Guichen Bay (Robe). In addition, over 400 women had been taken from the Central Depot, 'many by friends', wrote Moorhouse, and others by private individuals. He explained that he had advertised in the *Government Gazette* of 30 July 1855 that people not near a depot in the country could apply to him and one or two servants would be sent at government expense to any place 'on line of the mail road'. (This notice was printed in every *Gazette* until April 1856.) Overall a total of 810 had been 'taken'. However 240 had been returned, seventy-seven from country depots and 163 from the Adelaide Depot.[1]

There had been an Immigration Board, unpaid, since 1850. It consisted of the Immigration Agent, the Collector of Customs, and the Stipendiary Magistrate at Port Adelaide. In 1854 the Inspector of Police at the Port was also appointed.[2]

On the front cover note of Moorhouse's 24 September letter, Governor MacDonnell scribbled to Finniss that this proposal was the consequence of

> my suggestion. As the members of the Board will probably have to approve of some severe measures I thought it would be better to have a majority of Irishmen on the Board, paid a guinea for each attendance.

Consequently Major O'Halloran, Reverend Michael Ryan and Mr Kingston were requested to act as a board for the next six months, or for longer if necessary. Moorhouse had proposed that the board remain in office as long as the depot contained one hundred inmates and that it should be given the powers 'only to make such rules and regulations as the Gov may approve of'.[3]

Who were the members of this board? Why were they chosen? Presumably it would have been difficult for them not to accept the Governor's request that the majority of board members have Irish heritage. It is possible to illustrate their values and their attitudes to the girls for whose futures they were responsible by scrutinising the decisions they made. These men may have all been Irish, but they had very little in common, as a brief biographical sketch of each will illustrate.

Major Thomas Shuldham O'Halloran, born in India in 1797, came from a family with a long-established military background. He had sold his army commission (the purchase of English army commissions was not abolished until 1871) and in 1838 sailed for South Australia on the *Rajasthan* to settle on four sections at O'Halloran Hill. In June of that year Governor Gawler appointed him the first Police Commissioner. He led several expeditions to capture Aboriginals, the most famous being against the tribe which had murdered at least fifteen survivors of the wrecked *Maria* in 1840. A court martial, ordered by Gawler, resulted in two men being hung in the presence of their tribe. Matthew Moorhouse, the Protector of Aborigines at the time, was not present at either the trial or the executions. It would be interesting to know of the private opinions held at that time by both O'Halloran and Moorhouse of these events – particularly as the two men were to work closely together fifteen years later. O'Halloran resigned in 1841 as Police Commissioner when Governor Grey wanted him to accept the additional responsibility of acting as Police Magistrate. He was one of the four persons, not holding public office, chosen by Grey for the newly created Legislative Council in 1843. He failed to win the seat for Noarlunga in the Legislative Council when elections were held in 1851, did not stand for the 1855 elections, but was re-elected to the council in 1857. He has been described as a popular figure, a substantial farmer and horse breeder.[4]

His military background and his membership of the Church of England were sometimes reflected in the decisions he made as a board member. At one meeting, a request was considered from the Catholic girls in the Adelaide Depot for a substitute for meat to be provided during the season of Lent, and on the days when Church regulations required them to abstain from 'animal food'. Not surprisingly the board refused, O'Halloran pointing out that 'it was not done for soldiers'. On another occasion the board discussed whether the name of a doctor who was overcharging depot residents should be made public. O'Halloran said that military men were often called upon to perform disagreeable duties but could not refuse, and that the board was acting in an official capacity, however unpleasant. In this case, his argument was not accepted and newspapers did not publish the doctor's name.[5]

In 1854 O'Halloran was Chairman of the Brighton District Council. He had been the first president of the St Patrick's Society, which was established in 1849 and included prominent pioneers such as Robert Torrens and George Kingston. The St Patrick's Society promoted Irish immigration. It encouraged the recruitment of pauper girls as farm labourers after 1852 when the discovery of gold interstate had caused a dramatic exodus of hopeful miners from the colony. O'Halloran's brother William was the Auditor General from 1851 to 1868. O'Halloran was some times referred to as Colonel, other times as Major in the press.

George Strickland Kingston, architect and engineer, born in Cork in 1807 or 1808, arrived in South Australia on the *Cygnet* in 1836. He was one of the pioneer colonists, initially appointed Deputy Surveyor General, assistant to Colonel Light. It was commonly believed that he resigned in 1838 because Governor Gawler would not appoint him Surveyor General. He was the architect for the new Government House and was contracted to design the original section of the Adelaide Gaol. As a privately employed architect he was responsible for many significant buildings such as Ayers House, Cummins House and, of course, his own Kingston House. In 1844 he was a census collector, and later was employed as a surveyor for the proprietors of Burra who had requested a special survey. He was an original and large shareholder, later chairman of the South Australian Mining Association, responsible for the Burra Burra Monster Mine. In 1851 he was elected to the Legislative Council as the member for Burra and argued strongly for a fully elected bicameral parliament and secret ballot. A Freemason, he was vehemently opposed to state aid for church schools. In 1857 he was unanimously elected to the position of first Speaker of the new House of Assembly. Several contemporary descriptions indicate that he was unpopular; anonymously described as 'hollow hearted, empty headed and a treacherous fellow', and historian Douglas Pike has suggested Kingston's greatest attribute was his readiness to quarrel.[6] Nevertheless, he cannot have been too unpopular as he was re-elected Speaker in 1865.

Reverend Michael Ryan, born in Galway, arrived in Australia in 1838, and was initially based in Sydney. He was appointed assistant to the Catholic Bishop Francis Murphy in Adelaide in 1844, when he was in his mid thirties. Soon after arriving in

South Australia he spent some months in Clare, then began constant missionary tours to many areas in the colony to conduct services and carry out baptisms and marriages. He regularly visited Guichen Bay and the South East, travelling down to Mount Gambier, as well as to the Mount Barker District. He was appointed to the Destitute Board when it was first established in 1849. His knowledge of colonial conditions would, no doubt, have been considered of particular value when he was appointed to the Female Immigration Board (FIB).[7]

The two *ex-officio* members of the board, Matthew Moorhouse and Handasyde Duncan, the Immigration Agent, were both graduates in medicine, and neither was Irish.

Matthew Moorhouse was born in England in 1813, qualified as a surgeon in London in 1836 and practised in Hanley, where he became associated with Ridgeway Newland, a congregational minister. Moorhouse arrived in the colony in 1839 aboard the *Sir Charles Forbes* as a member of Newland's party, which went to Encounter Bay. Moorhouse was accompanied by his sister, Jane, and by his fiancee's brother, Henry Kilnor (sic). His brother, Ebenezer, arrived the next year, followed by Mary Kilner whom he married in 1842. It can be assumed, therefore, that he was optimistic about the prospects of this new colony. Before he left England it was recommended that he be appointed the Protector of Aborigines, and this position was confirmed within weeks of his arrival in 1839[8]. His initial salary was £250 per annum, and he quickly established a Native Location, comprising a school and hospital near the River Torrens. He was involved in several incidents in the 1840s, including the Rufus River Massacre when he accompanied a relief expedition to protect overlanders and stock from hostile Aborigines. Moorhouse was unable to prevent a confrontation, which resulted in the death of thiry-five Aborigines. His absence from the execution of the two Natives found guilty of the murder of the survivors of the wrecked brigantine *Maria* provoked much public and media discussion. After some years he published a book about the grammatical structure and vocabulary of the language spoken by the tribes of the River Murray, which indicates a commitment to his role as Protector. However, by 1855 he had only nominal duties as Protector and his role had no impact on his involvement with servant girls. He became a member of the Destitute Board in 1851 and was appointed Comptroller of the Destitute Poor Establishment in January 1855. His instructions were to take 'entire charge' and he was paid an additional salary of £100 per year.[9] The Destitute Board met once a fortnight and members were not paid. Initially the Immigrant Depot was administered as part of the Destitute Asylum, until the Female Immigration Depot (FID) was established.

Moorhouse resigned from all his government positions, including that of Protector of Aborigines, at the end of March 1856, for reasons unstated. Perhaps he was exhausted by the heavy workload and the vicissitudes of his duties. Nevertheless, he continued on occasions to act in a voluntary capacity as Comptroller for several months. Later he travelled with his family to England and attended the remarriage of his widowed sister, Jane, who had returned home after only a few years in the colony. His promotion of South Australia was acknowledged by his appointment, in April 1858, as the Immigration Agent in London. Later he returned to the colony and was elected as a member for Adelaide in the House of Assembly in 1860, retiring after two years. He later became a pastoralist and died on his property at Melrose, 'Bartagunyah', in 1876. Matthew Moorhouse was a complex man, often the centre of much public controversy[10].

Handasyde Duncan, a Scottish doctor of medicine, was born in 1811, and was twenty-nine when he arrived in Adelaide. He became a member of many boards, including the Destitute Board, and the first Board of Education. His duties as

Immigration Agent were to ensure immigrants were properly treated on board ship, and he was responsible for their reception, assistance with accommodation and employment. He was required to send quarterly reports to the Colonial Land and Emigration Commission in London. The accuracy of his assessments about the labour needs of the colony was evidenced in the 'Report of the Select Committee on Excessive Female Immigration'.

The first meeting of the board was held on Saturday, 6 October 1855. The duties, outlined by the Governor, were to:

1. frame regulations for the maintenance of proper discipline in the Adelaide and rural depots
2. create regulations relating to diet, cleanliness and sanitary precautions
3. establish the best means of transporting to and from country depots, to be responsible for the selection of matrons and to suggest places for settling the Immigrants to facilitate their absorption into the general population
4. recommend such expenditure as may be necessary to provide clothing, bedding, or other articles absolutely required for the use of the Immigrants
5. suggest the most economical means for depots to procure rations and supervising general expenditure
6. devise means to improve the knowledge of immigrants of domestic service and if possible for occupying them in industrial pursuits until they can find employment in service.[11]

The board sat six times in the first two weeks in order to create the necessary rules and regulations, after having first obtained approval from the Governor for such frequent meetings. After that the board met twice weekly until mid February 1856. No minutes are available so the operations of the board in the first few months became public only when issues were raised in the Legislative Council. Members of the press were eventually allowed to attend and report on meetings at the end of 1855.

Initial decisions reflected concern for the welfare of the residents of all the depots. In November the Female Immigration Board (FIB) put in a request to the Colonial Secretary for clothes. No doubt to ensure that money was granted, the board explained that no girl was to be supplied who had been less than four months in the colony and cases were to be considered on their merit.[12]

The most significant decisions made concerned the fate of those girls who had left a depot for service and were then 'disengaged'. The history of every depot illustrates the pivotal role taken by the board in determining who was eligible for readmission.

In March 1856 Colonial Secretary Finniss wrote to Moorhouse acknowledging his memo that the board's term was nearly expired and asking the board to continue till the end of April, noting the 'fast diminishing numbers now supported by Government'.[13] The *Adelaide Times* reported that Moorhouse attended all April meetings gratuitously as he had resigned from all his government positions.[14]

The final board meeting was held on 26 April 1856. There were 125 girls in the Adelaide Depot, and forty in country depots. An account for the payment of country doctors to attend the women there was itemised. Members thanked the Governor for his support and encouragement. As would be expected, no reference was made to threats of resignation over the management of the Willunga Depot or heated disputes like those over readmission policy. The depot was reported to be in 'a state of perfect order and cleanliness, its inmates vastly reduced in numbers, generally healthy and likewise tractable, obedient and respectful in their conduct'.[15] In reply the Governor applauded the board for its impartiality in carrying out 'trying and onerous' duties. The board had earlier acknowledged Moorhouse's service as he was 'no longer a governmental servant'.[16]

At this last meeting Patrick Ennis, described alternatively as the Overseer of the depot or as the Yard Supervisor, was given a 'certificate of good conduct' to assist him in finding employment.

Statistics provided early in May 1856 indicated that well over 2200 girls had been in the depot since the board had been established. Figures presented to the board at its last sitting illustrate the activities of the board[17] (see Appendix 2), and other figures provided earlier in the year for the Select Committee[18] indicate the number sent from the Central Depot to each country depot by 28 January 1856 (see Appendix 3). In summary and allowing for discrepancies in the figures quoted in different archival sources, approximately 750 girls had been sent to country depots by the end of January and by the end of April 450 had been placed. In the intervening months the Kapunda Depot had been established, and when the FIB disbanded, there were still three country depots operating, although two were in the process of closing. A few more girls, undoubtedly, were placed after April from both the Central Depot and those in Mount Barker, Encounter Bay and Kapunda, but the exact figure is not determinable.

How then had the country depots developed? Did the establishment of the FIB facilitate management of the single women and their placement? How did the Irish female immigrants react to being sent to depots in remote areas in the colony? Ellen was one of those sent to the Clare Depot and placed long before the board was created. The story of each country depot is told in the subsequent chapters, in the order in which they were established. The first to be opened, just a few weeks earlier than Clare, was in Willunga.

CHAPTER FIVE

Willunga: A Chairman Repulsed

Local Aboriginal clans are said to have named the area 'Willa-unga' – the 'place of green trees' – and it was one of the earliest settlements in the new colony. The first land survey of the Willunga District was supervised by John McLaren in 1839, after which property was quickly purchased and occupied. Aspiring wheat, sheep and cattle farmers then cleared their holdings of many of the green trees. A cottage, known as Government Hut, and three buildings – a post office, police station and survey office – were hastily erected by the Colonial Government on land known as the Government Reserve. This reserve was a meeting place, used as a tentage area for immigrants, and a government supply depot.

The journey from Adelaide to Willunga took six hours on horseback, and the township was a stopping place for travellers en route to Encounter Bay. Police were required to protect shipments travelling overland by bullock cart between Goolwa and Adelaide and to prevent coastal smuggling. In 1840 slate was discovered, resulting in an influx of Cornish quarrymen, increasing the population. A passenger and mail service between Willunga and Adelaide was established in that same year. By 1847 there was a resident schoolteacher at the Buckland House Academy and by 1851 two resident doctors. According to the 1855 census the District of Willunga had a population of 2474. By this time there were flour mills and a flax mill as well as a road to nearby Port Willunga. There were two licensed hotels in the town: the Bush Inn, built in 1839, and the Cornwall Inn.

As in most country areas in the new colony, the Wesleyan Chapel was the first church built. In Willunga it was erected in 1843, and enlarged just five years later. The foundation stones of St Stephen's Church of England and of St Joseph's Catholic Church were both laid in 1848. In 1852 the entire Catholic population, which was very small apparently, went to the gold fields, so that when Father Hughes took charge of St Joseph's in 1853 there had been no priest for nearly a year and no congregation! A Bible Christian chapel was opened in that same year and was in constant use until it later amalgamated with the Wesleyan church.[1]

At the time, then, that the first servants depots was established, Willunga was a thriving, well-established, church-going community.

A letter from Colonial Secretary Finniss, addressed to the Superintendent of the Female Immigration Depot (FID), Matthew Moorhouse, dated 9 July, requested that forty female immigrants be conveyed immediately to Willunga, under the charge of a superintendent and matron. To supervise the journey Moorhouse sent Richard Tapley, who was Relieving Officer at the Destitute Asylum and had been secretary to the Destitute Board at its inaugural meeting in 1849. The Matron was Ann Ennis, who remained until 19 September. The immigrants were to take cooking and mess utensils together with clothes and bedding for permanent residence. Finniss advised Moorhouse that

> the new building erected for a court house and police station will be ready for occupation on the 11th inst'. Arrangements were to be made with several tradesmen in the neighbourhood for the supply of rations, meat and other necessities, each article to be furnished, if possible, by a different tradesman.[342]

Today the National Trust maintains the original buildings along with the stables, the verandah and other rooms which were added later.

The District Council Chairman, Smith Kell, had written to the Colonial Secretary a few days earlier to advise that he had put twenty bunks in the court house for £16, and that Mr Hughes, the Catholic priest, had said that he would 'undertake for the girls' good conduct'.[3] However the girls arrived earlier than expected, and had to be given potatoes as bread had not yet arrived. (There was no bakery at Willunga at that time.) There was no table – one had been ordered to specific measurements and construction was not yet finished – nor were there forms for seating. The very new, unfinished, Willunga Depot was certainly not a warm comfortable refuge for displaced, unwanted females who had immigrated in anticipation of promised work. Nor were all the girls well clothed. In September Kell wrote to Moorhouse to say that thirty-two girls were barefoot and in need of shoes or boots.[4]

The journey from Adelaide to the depot was not uneventful for the girls. A bullock cart must have become bogged, or turned over, because Kell diligently attempted to recover two missing boxes. A correspondent to a daily paper wrote in January of the next year: 'Every traveller to Willunga shall risk his life by driving down a break-neck hill and then travel along a flat which is sometimes under water in winter.'[5]

Every effort was made to procure employment for the girls. Governor MacDonnell advised: 'The girls are to be allowed to accept any terms of hire they please; but are not to be permitted to refuse any offer of employment from persons whose respectability there is no reason to doubt.'[6]

Kell, in a letter to Moorhouse, only a week after they had arrived, reported that

> the girls are going off slowly which I cannot help attributing in

> a great measure to the impediments thrown in the way by the Reverend J. Hughes. He will insist on high wages, in no case under 4/- per week.

Hughes had also introduced a book to be signed by the employer, which gave the girls the right to attend Mass every alternate Sunday. The Governor was adamant that no girl should be readmitted who had refused employment with wages of 2/6 per week and meals for three months. He advised his Colonial Secretary to write to the Roman Catholic Bishop, Murphy, asking him to take such measures as may prevent, in future, Mr Hughes's unreasonable interference. He was confident of His Lordship's cooperation.[7] Bishop Murphy duly wrote to Father Hughes later that month, enclosing a copy of the letter from the Governor. The Bishop was highly appreciative of the priest's piety and zeal, but asked him not to become involved in matters such as employment.[8] The priest's efforts to establish a minimum wage were thus stymied.

An article in the *Register* of 2 August illustrates local attitudes – as well as the art of saying nothing while implying a great deal.

> We have recently received several complaints from the Willunga district of some local interference with the female Immigrants in the depot there, which prevents them from being hired out to the settlers. As we know that representations have been made in the proper quarter, and that measures have been taken to prevent, as far as possible, the recurrence of anything of the kind, we think it unnecessary to say more at present. The number of girls sent down from Adelaide to the Willunga depot was thirty-nine. Seventeen of these have taken situations for three months certain at wages averaging about 4/- a week, with board and lodging; and the remainder would probably soon meet with similar engagements but for the interference complained of.

Apparently Father Hughes had not been entirely unsuccessful in securing reasonable wages.

According to the evidence of Ann Ennis, a witness to the Select Committee, she was Matron of Willunga Depot from July to September. She was then sent by Moorhouse to the depot in town, after a disturbance in the Adelaide FID.[9] Her replacement at Willunga was Matilda Eliza Lewis. After the arrival of the new Matron, an incident occurred at the Willunga Depot which created much scandal. So strong was the public turmoil that the Legislative Council ordered, in January of the next year, that the correspondence between the Willunga District Council and the government on the subject of the single females sent to the Willunga Depot be printed.

The story could be used as the basis of a script for a period piece TV drama, with components of religious bigotry, threatened violence, harassment, and worker's rights or lack thereof, against a background of a country town in a fledgling colony.[10]

Smith Kell, Chairman of the District Council, wrote to Moorhouse, as superintendent of the FID, on 10 October.

> I am sorry to report that this morning there was a great disturbance at the depot, so much that I was obliged to call in the police. The dispute arose in consequence of my having forbidden them to go to a distance in the country, returning at all hours of the night without leave. After peace was restored, there was still one girl, of the name of Catherine Leary, whose conduct it would be impossible to overlook. She not only attempted to assault me at the time, but threatened to murder me the next time I came to the depot. I must, therefore, insist on her being recalled to Adelaide by the next mail.

Police had reported to Kell, whilst he was writing, that that the majority of girls at the depot were 'fully bent on a row, threatening every person who contradicts them'.

Matron Lewis' account was somewhat different. She reported on 11 October that two girls had been hired

> by going to see their fellow girls ... Mr Kell tried to prevent them going to see one another, but they paid no attention to him, or me, and he was obliged to call in the police to quiet them. The young people were home in time to answer to their names. I should feel greatly obliged if I had your permission for them, to either go or stay, to see one another.

Both letters were tabled at the next meeting of the newly created Female Immigration Board (FIB), which agreed to send copies to each correspondent, no doubt hoping to settle a misunderstanding. The board requested further information from Kell, and at the same time refused to recall Catherine Leary to Adelaide.

Mr Kell was 'quite unprepared for such rebuff'. For full particulars he referred the board to 'Corporal Richards, of the Police, or any other Protestant in the neighbourhood'. He said he would never enter the depot again, and was quite sure that 'neither the Governor, or the public, will allow me to be used in this manner'.

Matron Lewis's response to the copy of Kell's letter sent to her by the board was even stronger.

> I am very sorry that your mind should be so much disturbed with such barefaced falsehoods. What I stated I would declare on a *death-bed* ... the Corporal made use of a profane expression, and said that he would get them out of this place, or he would get himself out ... Three of the poor girls walked yesterday, barefooted, about sixteen miles, between the hours of ten and four, to get a situation. Mary Cain will leave today, at five shillings per week and the other two expect to be sent for this week. My husband gave Mary Cain an old pair [of boots] to enable her to go to her situation.

Matron Lewis was clearly affronted by the allegations that her residents were returning 'at all hours of the night', implying that she was not able to maintain control. The three girls she mentioned were obviously very anxious to leave the depot where they had been kept, possibly for several months, waiting to be employed. Matron implied that it was desperation that motivated all of those who walked, barefoot, over barely identifiable tracks to visit isolated farms. They would have been moving through a completely unfamiliar Australian bush, probably frightened by lizards, snakes, kangaroos and echidnas, to seek positions.

Mr Kell did indeed write, as he had threatened, to the Governor.

> Although I do not value the opinion of the Board, yet as I am anxious Your Excellency's mind should be disabused on the subject, I take the liberty of writing the following explanation.

He described how he had been surrounded and threatened by the girls so violently that he had to call for police assistance. The girl Catherine Leary had clearly upset him. 'She not only threatened to injure me if she could get at me then, but also declared her determination to do so the next morning if I came to the depot.' He felt the disturbance had been caused by his forbidding them to move freely out of the depot. Some of the girls had gone a distance of fifteen miles into the country and he had told them they should not go so far without his knowledge. He did not object to them visiting their friends in the neighbourhood, with Matron's permission. However he had been told his only business was to find them rations, 'that Mr (Father) Hughes was their master and he only would they obey'.

> Another cause of disturbance arose from my having allowed the Protestant girl to return to the depot after having been at

> service. I did so in consequence of her mistress proving out of her mind, and it being unsafe for her to remain.

Indeed, Matron had reported on 11 October that Mr Kell had given permission to readmit Eliza Shaw because her mistress was insane, but that she was now employed at 5/- per week. Kell claimed that Matron's letter to the Immigration Board 'is a great suppression of the facts … this can be proved by the police and myself, and others should Your Excellency wish it'.

The Colonial Secretary Finniss's response to the board's submission to the Governor of all correspondence and minutes relating to the disturbance was, perhaps unintentionally, provocative – and led to explosive results. Finniss reported that he was directed by the Governor to say that His Excellency had always found Mr Kell a useful and honourable assistant who had gratuitously exerted himself greatly, and put himself to great trouble in getting up the depot, at His Excellency's personal request. Mr Kell

> had good reason for considering that he has been held up to public obloquy by the Reverend Catholic Clergyman in the neighbourhood; whose conduct His Excellency felt it to be his duty to bring to the notice of the Right Reverend Bishop Murphy.

Finally, it seemed to the Governor that the Willunga Depot ought to be broken up: 'the girls there appear to be hired very slowly, and ought to be dispersed elsewhere.' The Governor's advice was heeded. Tables show that fifty-nine girls had been sent from the Central Depot by 24 September.[11] None were sent after the disturbance in October.

The reply from the board, dated 27 October, was immediate. The non-official members felt that the Governor's approval of Kell, who had refused to give the explanation requested by the board, was a direct censure of their proceedings. It was impossible for them to continue in an office, 'in which were Your Excellency's regulations to be carried out, we should have to issue orders to one who had already set our authority at defiance'. A few days earlier the FIB had instructed Matron that, as Mr Kell had 'given up' her establishment, she was to act in concert with the Reverend Hughes until further notice.

There was another issue of contention. Moorhouse had sent out rules and regulations to the matrons of the country depots when they were first established early in July. The newly created board drafted a more detailed, updated version and this had been forwarded to the Governor for his approval on 22 October. A modification suggested by MacDonnell to Rule No. 8 was not at all radical but board members could not see how they could operate under his amendment at the Willunga Depot. He had proposed that the clerical visitors were to attend at times agreed upon by the Superintendent, rather than by the Matron, as the board had stated.[12] This proposal undoubtedly presented the board with a quandary. If the Chairman of the District Council refused to manage the depot and no Superintendent had been appointed, then who was going to be responsible for supervising clerical visits, if not the Matron? The non-official members therefore tendered their resignations unless the Governor would withdraw his letters and confirm Rule No. 8 as originally submitted.

The Colonial Secretary's reply to the threat of resignation was, this time, more tactful. Finniss restated the Governor's views but acknowledged board members' anger by agreeing to reconsider Rule No. 8. His Excellency, he wrote, learnt with great surprise that the board considered that he had expressed approval of Mr Kell's manner towards the board. 'His Excellency is not aware that he expressed *any opinion whatsoever.*'

He had simply stated

> what he personally knew of Mr Kell's previous gratuitous exertions ... Mr Kell, appealing to Protestant testimony, did so in consequence of the interference of the Roman Catholic Clergyman in that district, whose conduct contrasted, in His Excellency's opinion, unfavourably with that of his fellow clergy. Having thus discharged the simple duty of stating what he knew of Mr Kell, and having added his own opinion in favor of breaking up the depot, His Excellency left the Board free to act in the matter as they chose; and, he cannot, therefore, suppose the Board really asks the Governor of the Colony to withdraw a letter containing his personal testimony of facts ...

The Governor assumed that members of the board were speaking of resignation because of the importance they attached to Rule No. 8. He was prepared, therefore, to give further consideration to the matter and hoped that no inconvenience would result 'as the Board is now perfectly unfettered in regard to the management of the Willunga Depot'.

Nevertheless, on 3 November the Governor agreed to cancel or destroy all the correspondence relating to the Willunga dispute and Rule No. 8. Resignations were consequently withdrawn.[13] The FIB had been in existence less than three weeks when the non-official members threatened to resign. The Governor's desire to avoid any obvious bias against Irish female immigrants by appointing three Irishmen to the board had produced a most unexpected outcome. The board, in protecting and defending the feisty servant girls, had successfully asserted its authority to oversee the management of the Willunga Depot, and by implication, all other depots. The exertions of the local Catholic priest had inadvertently contributed to this outcome.

It is not clear whether the FIB or the Governor made the final decision about Rule No. 8. Moorhouse wrote to the Colonial Secretary on 13 November requesting approval for the printing of 200 copies of the rules. 'It was agreed that Rule 8 should be expunged from the Rules for the Country Depots.'[14] There was no further comment.

The event also raised interesting legal issues. The Corporal in Charge, Richards, in his report of the incident on 10 October to George Hamilton, Senior Inspector of Police in Adelaide, said Mr Kell 'was repulsed by the females from the place' and so called for assistance. He did not know what would happen if the incident should re-occur and any arrest be necessary – 'they are such a determined lot'. His understanding of the cause was 'Mr Kell's interference with the Girls for visiting those who had left for service, also fearing they might fall in with improper company'. Police Commissioner Warburton submitted this report to the Governor for his information. He asked for guidance in dealing with the women.

> It is not clear under whose authority and orders the police would be justified in using force … nor whether a breach of Depot Regulations, unaccompanied by a breach of the peace, would subject any of these women to Legal penalties.

The Advocate General was asked to advise and there were complex legal opinions expressed about the right of district councillors to interfere. According to one opinion, normal police powers were limited to prevention of a breach of the peace, and the arrest of any person guilty in his presence of an assault.[15]

It was stated in the *Government Gazette* on 13 November 1855 that Willunga Depot would be closed from 1 January 1856. Expenses for the depot, including rent and transport, but not including food, clothing and furniture, or Matron's salary, was listed in the 'First Report of the Select Committee', as being £337-7-8. The report stated that a total of sixty-one girls had been sent from the Central Depot. It is not known if any girls were removed to other depots when Willunga closed but evidence confirms that the depot did close at the nominated date. Matron Lewis was paid for December[16] and it was recorded at the FIB meeting on 26 January 1856 that she had returned to Adelaide. In January the depot became a police station.

CHAPTER SIX

Clare: A Successful Enterprise

The township of Clare in 1855 was a developing service centre, providing farm produce and timber for the nearby mining communities. It was a stopping place for the bullock drays hauling copper ore from Burra to Port Wakefield along the Gulf Road and for those using the main route to the north of the colony. Clare's male population was 516 according to the census of 1855. There was a police station, a court house, a Catholic church (St Michael's) with an attached school, an Anglican church, a local doctor, at least two inns, a post office and a mail service. There was a higher proportion of Catholics in the population of the Clare Valley than in other areas where depots were established. A Wesleyan chapel, usually the first church building established in newly settled areas, was not opened in Clare until 1857.

Four years earlier the District Council of Clare had been established with E.B. Gleeson, an Irishman, elected as first Chairman. The village had been laid out by Gleeson on property near his homestead 'Inchiquin'. Robert Noye, in his history of Clare, wrote: 'It was not until 1846 that the name Clare appeared, in which year addresses were recorded as Clare Village or Clareville.'[1] Gleeson remained a central figure in the valley, becoming the first Mayor when Clare became a corporation in 1868. The District Clerk, William Lennon, an Irish Catholic, was a former schoolteacher who had opened and taught at the first school in Clare, attached to St Michael's Church. He was elected to the House of Assembly in 1860 at the same time as Matthew Moorhouse, but resigned in 1861 because he was insolvent. Lennon was opposed to the later resumption of assisted immigration, no doubt influenced by his experiences with the Clare Depot.

Mary Ann Keenan was appointed Matron of the Clare Depot and paid 3/- per diem from 23 July 1855. A house, to be the depot, was rented for £1 per week from the same date[2] from Mr Kingsmith.[3] Unfortunately the location of the house cannot be determined from the records in the archives of the Lands Titles Office.

Richard Tapley, the Relieving Officer at the Destitute Poor Establishment, told the Legislative Council Select Committee that he had been requested to go and establish country depots. 'I always went with the first party of girls sent out to country districts, and made the necessary local arrangements for lodging and parties to take charge of them.'[4]

Initially, conditions would not have been comfortable in this depot. A letter from the Matron written early in August apologised for her bad writing as she had no table, and requested a new ration book as she had lost most of her papers 'in the wet'. She had to meet many unexpected expenses, as the journey from Adelaide had taken two nights. Accommodation of sorts had to be found for her and the girls she was accompanying on drays. Matron asked that arrangements be made to send on her hempen basket which had been left behind at the German Hospital. 'There were many things in it which would be useful hear (*sic*). In fact I could not replace the same articles for 2 pounds', and she expected to be reimbursed if the basket was lost. Not having access to valued possessions that had been carefully selected for use in a new colony must indeed have been disappointing. The restricted budget did not help. She asked to be allowed to spend a shilling a day on meat 'as they do in Adelaide', presumably for each girl.[5] Attempts were made by the local community to ease conditions. Gleeson wrote to Moorhouse early in September informing him that some girls arrived at the Clare Depot without blankets 'but were immediately supplied'. Two girls had left theirs at the German Hospital, one thinking that she was not entitled to hers, the other thinking she would be supplied with one at Clare.[6]

Two days after Matron and the girls had arrived, William Lennon had written to the Colonial Secretary. He reported, with some umbrage, that seven female immigrants could have got employment on arrival with respectable settlers for 2/6 a week plus board and lodgings but Matron Keenan advised them not to accept as she considered the wages too low. He had told the new arrivals that the government would not keep them in the depot to 'suit their own fancy in situations', and suggested that Matron be requested not to interfere with wages offered.[7] Matthew Moorhouse had already drawn up 'Rules for the Immigrants at Country Depots'. Rule No. 5 stated that 'no person shall be permitted to remain in the depot if she refuse any respectable situation'. In a letter to the Colonial Secretary, Moorhouse enclosed a printed copy of these rules with a handwritten note attached.

> These are the regulations under which the matron at Clare is acting – No. 5 is sufficiently explicit and she evidently did wrong in expressing any opinion about wages – I cannot justify it and wd dismiss her if His Excellency shd consider it ought to be done.[8]

He advised that this regulation had been laid 'pointedly before the Clare matron'. Consequentially, Matron Keenan had rapidly to alter her advice. The *Adelaide Observer* reported in August that

> Up to this morning twenty of the servants [at Clare] depot will go off in the course of the week. They are a fine healthy lot of girls and give great satisfaction to their employers who speak very highly of them.[9]

A few days later a letter from the Lennon reported that thirty girls had been placed and thirty more were required. 'Girls who have left the depot are being well spoken of by their employers and in several cases wages have been already advanced.'[10]

Matron listed twenty girls employed by 5 August with details of each employer's name and address and the salary paid. All except Hannah Neal were engaged for six months.

Ellen Moore, after surviving the shock of shipwreck and accommodation in two ad hoc facilities prior to a long, uncomfortable, wet trip to a sparse building in a very small country town, was one of the first girls to be employed. She was hired as a domestic servant by Mrs McKenzie, an inn keeper, for 2/6 per week. Nothing remains today of McKenzie's hotel, the Stanley, known as the 'Travellers Rest', but presumably staff facilities were adequate.

Ellen, along with all the other girls in this first group sent to Clare, had been taken to the depot directly from the German Hospital where there were still, at the end of June, many passengers from the shipwreck. At least sixteen of the twenty names can be easily found on the *Nashwauk* passenger list. Matron Keelan's spelling is variable and her writing often indecipherable so the other four were very probably *Nashwauk* passengers as well. Her Ellen Connolly may have been Ellen Crowley. Similarly her Brigid Calligan may have been Bridget Kelleher (recorded on the German Hospital list as Kellingham) who had a sister, Susan, again recorded by Matron in September as Susan Calligan. There is one surname which is unreadable and may have referred to Mary Pigot although there is no Pigot listed at the German Hospital. Alternatively it may have referred to Mary Pearce, who is not listed on the passenger list but is recorded on the German Hospital list as being from the *Nashwauk*. There remains just one name, deciphered as Lucy Donovan, which is not recorded on the ship's passenger list. Matron lists only one girl named Lucy, so she was very probably referring to Lucy Hourigan, a *Nashwauk* passenger, employed on 30 July by Mr Harrison from Clare at 2/6 per week. She did record another Donovan, Eliza known as Bessie, from the *Nashwauk*, who was sent from the German Hospital to Clare, where she was engaged and paid 2/6 per week by Mrs Rowe.

A letter dated 2 September, from Matron to Moorhouse suggested that as some of the girls are 'not engaging as quick as at first ... [there] had better not be any more of the *Nashwalk* (*sic*) girls sent. I have sixteen girls disengaged now'.[11] She forwarded another list of girls engaged, again specifying the wages offered and the names and addresses of the employers. Careful perusal indicates that another sixteen are clearly recognisable from the *Nashwauk* passenger list and all but two, Margaret Green and Bridget Flaherty, had come to the Clare Depot from the German Hospital.

Matron's next letter, sent a week later, listed nine women engaged, this time including several from other ships. None were being paid less than 3/- per week, and one, Susan Kelleher (Calligan), a *Nashwauk* passenger, was receiving 5/-. Overall, during its first six weeks of operation, the Clare Depot secured employment for at least forty of the girls from the shipwreck.

Clearly the Clare Depot was proving successful. Early in September Gleeson reported, 'Fifty of the girls sent here are now in comfortable situations and are well spoken of' and a few days later gave a favourable report on the treatment of females at the depot.[12] Moorhouse, as Comptroller, on 24 September signed a list of figures relating to the country depots, which indicate that sixty-nine girls had been sent to Clare and sixty-two had been hired.[13]

The Clare Depot continued to facilitate employment. By the end of December it was reported at a Female Immigration Board (FIB) meeting that eight girls had been engaged for harvesting at 8/- per week, with the promise of subsequent situations and that only three remained. Board members noted that only a fortnight ago there had been thirty girls in the depot. Early in January Matron reported that she had refused to readmit three girls who had left their places 'of their own accord'.[14] They had found 'fresh' places much quicker than if they had been readmitted.

The Matron was identified as Mrs Quinlam in the *Register* at the end of December. Either her name was misheard by the reporter or a replacement for Ann Keenan had been hired temporarily, which would be most unlikely. Nor was any comment made about the whereabouts of Ann Keenan, if she had been replaced, but there is some evidence that she was ill. At the end of January, the FIB considered Matron Keenan's request for payment of her medical expenses and agreed that as all matrons were receiving wages paid by the government they should pay their own doctor's bills. Obviously not happy to be so easily dismissed, Ann Keenan wrote and asked the board to reconsider. She had been ill for two months as a direct consequence of over-exerting herself when transporting the girls up to Clare. The weather had been very bad and there was little food. They had needed to stay one night at the Saddleworth Hotel, for which she had paid out of her own pocket. Her bed had been damp and the next day she had to wade through mud for several miles.[15] The board quickly decided to pay the hotel bill, but not the medical expenses.[16] It was also agreed that, on the breaking up of depots, every matron's travel expenses to Adelaide should be paid but they should not be accommodated in the Adelaide Depot.[17]

A letter from Gleeson was considered by the FIB on 16 January. Only one girl was left at the Clare Depot and he considered it desirable to close the depot, 'as there does not appear to exist any demand for more'.[18] He wanted it to be published that 120 had been employed, all giving satisfaction to their employers. The board wrote to Gleeson saying that the depot could be closed as soon as possible.[19]

There were only a few disruptions to the management of the depot. Matron complained about two girls named Griffen who acted 'very indifferent', moving from place to place and who, when they left, had taken a shawl belonging to another girl, Ellen Collins.[20] Another situation was given some press coverage. At the FIB meeting on 26 January it was reported that Matron had locked out a girl, Ellen MacDonald, for her 'disreputable' behaviour. She had become too close to her master, Mr Spratt. From the evidence available it is not possible to determine whether or not this was the blacksmith, Thomas Spratt, who lived in Temple Road. Mrs Spratt had returned Ellen to the depot, yet Mr Spratt continued to see her. It was reported in the *Adelaide Times* that she was sent away on the mail coach[21] and there is a record of her transport costs being met by the Destitute Board.[22] No charges were laid against Mr Spratt and we do not know what happened to Ellen immediately after she was removed from the depot. She had been a nineteen-year-old *Nashwauk* passenger from Cork who had stayed at the German Hospital and been some time at the Destitute Asylum. In December the following year she married Thomas Edmunds of Kooringa at St Joseph's Church in Kooringa.[23] A daughter, Frances, was born in September 1860.[24]

Marriages of at least five girls from the *Nashwauk* who were sent to the Clare Depot were recorded in the Sevenhills Register of Marriages. One, Susan Kelleher (Kelcher? Calligan?), a nineteen-year-old from Clare who had been employed by Mr Bryden from near Skillogalee Creek married

Edward Nicholls of Skillogalee Creek in January 1856. A letter from Jean Turner, a descendant who lives in Novar Gardens, verifies that Susan was sister to Brigid, who also went to the Clare Depot.

Bridget Riordan, from Cork, who was recorded as being twenty on the *Nashwauk* passenger list, was only fifteen years old according to her descendants, John Tuohy and Denis Connell. There is no evidence that she was accompanied by anyone, although there may have been a married sister on board. Regulations, issued in October 1854, for the selection of emigrants and conditions on which passages for South Australia were granted, established by the Government Emigration Office in London, were very clear. 'Single women under 18 cannot be taken without their parents, unless they go under the immediate care of some near relative', so it is extremely unlikely that she would have been accepted as an unattached fifteen-year-old. It is possible that she lied about her age, but selection agents were required to confirm nominated age with written evidence, often a baptismal certificate, and the penalties for false representation were quite severe. Whatever her age, Bridget must have been a courageous young woman, optimistically prepared to sail away on a long journey in cramped conditions to an unknown land to seek employment and a husband. Soon after the ship was wrecked she experienced another trauma at sea. She had boarded the steamer *Melbourne* at Port Noarlunga with about seventy others to travel to Port Adelaide, but a deck railing collapsed and she fell overboard. She was rescued within a few minutes by several of the crew and, after landing, accommodated with the other passengers in the German Hospital.

It is assumed that she was the Bridget Redling (Matron's writing) who was sent to the Clare Depot and listed by Matron as having been engaged on 25 August by Mr Rogers, the schoolmaster at Clare. Eighteen months later Bridget married Jacob Von Haarsma who, according to family tradition, was one of her rescuers. He had been born in Holland in 1834. The couple married in the Wesleyan Chapel at Spring Farm, near Mintaro, on 30 March 1857. Bridget's name is spelt Readen and Jacob's is minus the Von in the Register of Marriages. A photograph of them in their wedding clothes seems to emphasise the seriousness of the occasion. Nine children were born, and the deaths of two are recorded, both a day old: Julia died in 1870 and Mary in 1867. Jacob also died at the young age of forty-one, at Sevenhills, in 1875. Bridget moved to Georgetown to be with one of her daughters, Bridget, who had married Denis McCarthy, and their family of nine children. Henrietta, one of Bridget's daughters, born in 1896, is believed to have stayed in Georgetown to care for her grandmother after her parents had shifted to Tailem Bend. Bridget Riordan is buried in the Georgetown cemetery, where her unmarked grave is tended by a great-grandson, Jack Vaughton. There is no registration of her death and no existing burial records to confirm the date but it is thought to be between 1914 and 1918.

According to the *Nashwauk* passenger list there were two Bridget Whites, both twenty-four years old, one from County Clare and one from Galway, and both stayed at the German Hospital. Both were recorded as being sent to Clare, one being employed in September for 3/- per week by Mr Evans from Auburn, the other employed for 4/- by Mr Beacon from near Broughton. One married John Cousin of Bungaree on 7 May 1856.

Catherine Coffey, twenty, a domestic servant from Kings, had been taken to the German Hospital. She was in the first group of girls to be sent to the Clare Depot, and was employed on 27 July by Mr Hitchcock, a saddler in Clare. In June 1858, she married Robert Henry of Armagh at Mr Butler's residence.

Another young woman, twenty-year-old Joanna Leary (O'Leary) from Cork, who stayed at the German Hospital, was employed from the Clare Depot in September by Mr Paul Tierck(?) near Wakefield for 3/- per week. She married Robert Giles of Kooringa in June 1856.

Brigid O'Brien, twenty-two, from County Clare, who had stayed at the German Hospital, was engaged by Mrs Burscott of Armagh for 2/6 per week. She married Benjamin Horne. A daughter, Ellen, was born in 1859 and several more children were born at Auburn.[25]

There was some sickness among the Irish girls sent to the district. In early 1856 Catherine Horgan (Hogan) became very ill and needed either to be shifted to Adelaide or provided with medical attention in the country. The board agreed that she was to be given medical attention at the home of her late employer, Mr McDermott.[26] Another illustration of the lack of nursing facilities in the country was provided when the cost of board and lodging for three weeks for a Margaret Ryan was paid to T. Fitzsimmons by order of Mr Gleeson.[27] In March, transport from Clare to the Adelaide Depot was arranged for her, again by Gleeson.[28] Presumably she was sufficiently recovered to be employed as she was returned to the servants depot and not to either the Adelaide Hospital or the Destitute Asylum. There is no record on the Matron's early lists of one of the two Margaret Ryans who were passengers on the *Nashwauk* being 'engaged' in Clare, but one may have been sent up to the depot later, when Matron was no longer required to provide lists. There is a record of a Mary Ryan, from the *Nashwauk* and the German Hospital, who was employed by Mr Hope, at that time Manager of the Bungaree Station near Clare, in September for 3/- per week. It was probably this Mary Ryan who was listed, amongst several others, as having received medical attention in the depot in the second half of 1855.[29]

Early in February, Matron was advised to remove the remaining girls and bedding to the newly established servants depot at Kapunda.[30] Matron reported to the FIB meeting on 9 February that there were no girls on rations but that numerous girls were returning to the depot thinking they would be sent on to the Adelaide Depot. As a result, four girls were sent from Clare to Kapunda, with boxes and cooking utensils.[31]

At the FIB meeting on 13 February it was noted that Matron Keenan objected to her dismissal without notice.[32] At the next meeting she asked permission to remain one week longer as she was indisposed, and reported that five girls had been requested. In response, the board stated that settlers should send requests for servants to the Central Depot.[33]

As a consequence several letters of complaint were tabled at the board meeting early in March. Girls who had been hired had not been sent. Moorhouse said he felt unauthorised, without the board's consent, to send girls to Clare, 'that neighbourhood having been so glutted with female servants'.[34]

Undoubtedly the Clare Depot had been highly successful in placing girls with local farmers. Figures quoted in the minutes of evidence for the Legislative Council Inquiry reported that 121 had been sent from the Central Depot to Clare by 28 January 1856.

Nevertheless, in mid March the board again declined to provide two servants – as the depot was closed.[35] Towards the end of that month another letter was received by the board from a Christopher Giles complaining about the closure of the Clare Depot. He had a need for servants, as did others, and the cost of transporting them from Adelaide was a quarter of the cost of the trip from England! The board suggested he apply to Kapunda where a new servants depot had been established, and noted that many Clare girls had been dismissed after harvest.[36] The Kapunda Depot had been created to provide a local facility for displaced girls and at the same time to provide labour to meet other regional demand.

CHAPTER SEVEN

Robe: Insubordination

Guichen Bay, named by the French explorer Nicolas Baudin, was selected as a shipping port for the squatters of the South East by the Lieutenant Governor Frederick Holt Robe, in 1846. On the shores of Guichen Bay, a town of fifty-two acres comprising quarter-acre lots was surveyed. A Government Resident arrived, town allotments were sold, and a medical officer was appointed. Robetown was proclaimed in 1847, a police station erected and a court house the next year. The Robe Telegraph Station was opened in July 1855. The 1855 census records the population of the district as 1209 with 532 in the township.

Father Michael Ryan, on a missionary journey from Adelaide to Mount Gambier, called in at Robe in 1853, two years before he was appointed to the Female Immigration Board (FIB). Construction of the first Catholic church was not begun until 1858.[1] An indenture was signed in October 1855 for the building of a Bible Christian chapel, to be used by all denominations. So it was in a very new settlement, without as yet a building for religious worship in an area known as 'the wastelands', that a servants depot was established in July 1855. It was not until the early months of the next year, at about the time the depot was closing, that ship-loads of Chinese gold miners started arriving, to then walk to Bendigo and Ballarat goldfields to avoid paying the £10 poll tax imposed by the Victorian Government.

Charles Brewer arrived in Adelaide in 1840 with his wife and four children, having sold his commission in the Royal Artillery. He brought out with him a wooden house, milch cow, and a Scottish shepherd and family.[2] However, he was unsuccessful as a farmer in the new colony and after about nine years he applied for a government position – in which he was also unsuccessful. Charles Brewer was dismissed as the Immigration Agent by order of the Secretary of State in London, Earl Grey, in 1850 as he had failed to make diligent investigations into many serious passenger complaints of ill treatment over several months.[3] Brewer then became the Government Resident and Stipendiary Magistrate at Robetown. Perhaps in this position he proved more competent, although he was not averse to disobeying government instructions! He lived in the heritage-listed 'Robe House' in Hagen Street.

A District Council was not formed until 1869 so it was to Charles Brewer that Governor MacDonnell's circular about the disposal of single female Irish immigrants was sent. Brewer's response was clear. 'I could not recommend the establishment of a depot in this district, especially of the class proposed.' He felt few servants were needed near Robetown. Nevertheless he suggested that, as there was no accommodation available at Robe, a small party could be sent, with plenty of publicity, and the girls could be employed directly on arrival. He reported that a Catholic priest suggested that perhaps twenty could be distributed in the Penola District.[4]

Despite Brewer's assessment of the area's employment capacity, on 28 July Richard Tapley arrived on the government schooner, *Yatala*, with eighty girls! Brewer, as Government Resident, had no choice but to oversee the establishment and operation of a Female Immigration Depot (FID). He immediately arranged for twenty girls, supervised by the Catholic priest, to be transported to Penola by dray, at a cost of 30/- per head. He advised the Governor that he would send ten girls to

Mosquito Creek (Struan) and ten to Mount Gambier as soon as he had confirmation of suitable lodgings. He contracted with a local businessman, George Ormerod, to erect a building for twenty-five to forty, pre-empting the Governor's approval.[5]

George Ormerod was a pastoralist with extensive property throughout the South East of the colony. His shipping company, Ormerod & Co., dealt with all exports and most imports at Port Robe.[6] Brewer arranged that the court house, police station, and one of Ormerod's wool stores be used to accommodate the girls whilst Ormerod had workmen build a barn-like structure of old ship's timber with a galvanised iron roof on the open land known as Section 16. The building included a lean-to kitchen and quarters for Matron. Ormerod was paid £25 for the first three months of occupation and then rent was 20/- per week.[7] It is probable that the wool store/depot was located on the present site of the Ormerod Cottages in Smillie Street.

Ormerod employed Robert Anderson as a carpenter whose wife, Isabella, became Matron of the Immigration Depot. Both had been passengers, with their two children, on the *Nashwauk* (their names are recorded as Aderson on the passenger list). Just a few weeks after the shipwreck Isabella was admitted, suffering from fever, to the Adelaide Hospital where she stayed for a month. Then, family historian Rob Anderson reports, in July her one-year-old daughter died. A week later she was responsible for the care of eighty young women for whom there was only ad hoc accommodation! As well as coping with the traumas of shipwreck, hospitalisation and the death of an infant, she was also pregnant. A son was born in September. Nevertheless, at the time the girls were still accommodated, no doubt very uncomfortably, in temporary locations, Brewer wrote that 'the conduct of the females here [Robetown] has been good with some exceptions' and that he was entirely satisfied with the Matron in charge 'whose task is very difficult'.[8]

In mid August 1855, Brewer advised the Colonial Secretary that eight female immigrants had been employed at £15 per year, twenty-four had been sent to Penola and forty-seven remained in Robe. Inspector Scott, at Penola, had reported that the twenty-four had arrived safely, a house had been rented at 10/- per week, and that he, in conjunction with Mr Powell, the Catholic priest, would superintend them until they procured situations. The cottage was rented for seventeen weeks, until mid November, and the Matron, Mary O'Keiff, was paid the same amount as all matrons at that time, £1 per week. Brewer had arranged for the reception of ten or twelve at Mosquito Plains near Naracoorte and at Mount Gambier.

It was also in August that the first reference to the District Surgeon, Mr Thomas Young Cotter was made. Brewer reported that Mr Cotter had been called in to deal with mostly trifling matters without Matron's knowledge, and that the girls were becoming very troublesome. He added that as a consequence Matthew Moorhouse was writing to Cotter.[9] The dispute between Brewer and Cotter, which inevitably involved much bureaucratic correspondence, continued for months. By December the Colonial Secretary was writing to Brewer to say that the Governor 'has every confidence in you' in regard to this medical officer.[10] Consequently, Cotter was replaced by Dr Penny in January.[11] In mid January 1856, the board received a letter from Dr Cotter saying that a girl had died in the town without any medical attention, clearly implying either neglect or incompetence by his replacement. The letter was sent to the Colonial Surgeon.[12] One of the Scottish Highlanders who had arrived in the town in October, Ann Campbell, had died of typhus and dysentery. Brewer reported that, upon inquiry, there was 'no neglect'.[13] By May the Governor had declined sanctioning payment to Cotter for services he had rendered to the girls in the servants depots, as they were considered unnecessary. Yet Dr Penny, of Guichen Bay, was paid over £50 for his services to the girls at Robetown.[14]

On 1 September 1855 Brewer reported that five girls had been hired at Penola and twelve had been sent to Mount Gambier. One girl, Bridget Mahey(?) had been so insubordinate that Brewer had expelled her from the depot. She had initially refused to go to Penola, which the Matron 'passed over', and afterwards was selected for Mount Gambier. On the morning the party left she had hidden herself away and did not make her appearance until night. 'Besides these two cases of opposition to orders Matron said her general conduct was very bad.' Brewer felt it necessary to expel her as an example to others.[15] There is no further reference to this Bridget. The consequences of being denied food and accommodation in a port town, with few facilities, far from the city, must have been horrifying.

A letter from Brewer was received in the Colonial Secretary's office later in September indicating that fourteen of the twenty-four sent to Penola had been engaged. 'Mrs Scott writes that the remaining ten are not likely to be very soon disposed of, as the neighbourhood appears to be fully supplied with servants.' Mrs Scott was the wife of the local Police Inspector. Another eight situations were found by Mrs McIntosh at Mosquito Creek and four at Mount Gambier.[16]

By mid October nineteen girls remained in the Robe Depot with little prospect of employment. Six weeks later the FIB stated that single women should be removed from Guichen Bay to Penola because of the slow rate (one a week) of hiring at Robetown.[17] A notice was subsequently published in the *Government Gazette* of 13 December that servants would be sent from Guichen Bay to Penola for the convenience of settlers in the interior. Clearly there had been no prior consultation with Brewer, because he, in response, reported that Inspector Scott had written that there was no place for girls to stay at

Penola. The house that had been hired as a depot was to be occupied by the owner and there were no other vacant houses available in the town. 'The twenty-four I'd sent were four months getting employment, the last girl having been engaged on the 6th of this present month.'[18] Brewer felt that work was just as likely to be found at Robe where there was, at least, suitable accommodation for the girls. He had not conveyed more females from Robe to Penola as directed by the FIB until he had informed members of this situation. Not surprisingly, the board considered Brewer's reasons 'satisfactory' and rescinded the order.[19]

Communicating by horse-carried mail was not only slow but often confusing. In the midst of this correspondence about a depot being no longer available, Mrs Anderson wrote to the board asking whether or not she should accompany two girls to situations in Penola or should Miss O'Keiff be requested to continue?[20] The board agreed that Miss O'Keiff should be maintained. But where, if there was no longer any depot at Penola? We can only presume that she lived in the town and was able to supervise transport to take the two girls already hired to their places of employment.

At an FIB meeting in mid February, it was noted that the Governor had recently inspected the Robe depot.[21] The *Register* reported that the Governor had embarked on the *Yatala* on 3 February, intending to visit Port Elliot, Guichen Bay and Port Lincoln.[22] Unfortunately there is no record available of his impressions.

After the Governor's visit two more girls were hired but still six awaited placement. Father Ryan thought it would be cheaper to pay the girls wages than to maintain the depot, so it was agreed the depot should be abolished. The Colonial Secretary was to advise the Matron and the girls were to be supervised by the person responsible for the Highlanders.[23] Twenty-eight[24] Gaelic-speaking Highland families (147 persons) had landed at Guichen Bay in October 1855, few speaking English.[25] In fact, as the former Matron Mrs Anderson pointed out, she and her husband were the people supervising the Highlanders!

The Robe Depot finally closed in March 1856 when Brewer asked that the remaining immigrants be sent back to town.[26] Three Irish girls were returned to the Adelaide Depot.[27] The vacated building was then used by Ormerod & Co.[28] as a bulk store.

Overall, seventy-seven of the eighty girls sent from the Central Depot were placed. Matron reported that some girls had been hired for twelve months, some for six months and none for less than three months.[29] Twelve girls were employed locally, ten went to Mosquito Plains, twenty-four to Penola and twelve to Mount Gambier, and the remainder to outlying stations, according to the Legislative Council Select Committee report. Brewer's initial assessment of the employment potential of this large district was remarkably accurate.

It is not possible to establish whether any girls from the *Nashwauk* were sent to Guichen Bay. Brigid Maher's behaviour may very well have been explained by a not unreasonable fear of the unknown, a fear no doubt shared by some other depot residents. Yet no other girls were expelled. Perhaps they were too frightened by Brewer's intolerance of insubordination to object to being sent to isolated destinations.

CHAPTER EIGHT

Gawler: No Mattresses

Gawler was one of the oldest towns in the colony and could be expected to have some stability and infrastructure to facilitate the establishment of a servants depots.

Colonel Light and his assistant B.T. Finniss had surveyed the Gawler District in 1839, and laid out the town into one hundred one-acre blocks with another 150 acres set aside for parklands, schools, churches and other community facilities. The town was on the main road from Kapunda to Port Adelaide, constructed in the early 1840s after the discovery of copper. William Duffield, the first Mayor, arrived in 1847 and purchased the flour mill. Three schools were recorded in the archives of 1850 and there was a petition for the appointment of a Stipendiary Magistrate in 1855. The first church, built in 1846, was Anglican. The small Catholic church was built in 1852.[1]

In 1854 the Mudla Wirra and Barossa West local government bodies were formed and Duffield was elected as a member of both, recorded as Chairman of Barossa West in 1856,[2] and as Chairman of Mudla Wirra in 1855.[3] Gawler Town was in the precincts of both Barossa West and Mudla Wirra councils and a separate town corporation was not formed until July 1857, the same year the railway from Gawler to Adelaide was opened. The journey from Adelaide to Gawler in 1855, when the servants depot was established, was still hazardous. 'Peril and danger was not infrequent from bad roads, swollen streams, jibbing horses and reckless drivers.'[4]

The Mudla Wirra District Council met in Mr Duffield's office in Gawler Town on Tuesday 3 July, and resolved to hold a special meeting in the old schoolroom. The public and the representatives of the Barossa West Council were to be invited to consider the Governor's circular about the excess of single, Irish, female immigrants. The meeting was held the following Monday and was well attended. It was resolved that the establishment of a permanent depot for both males and females would be beneficial to residents. A temporary Female Immigration Depot (FID) would be a first step towards achieving this goal. However, by the end of the month nothing had happened and the District Council wrote to the Colonial Secretary to ask why the girls had not been sent.[5] There are no other references at all to the depot in this council's minutes.

Records about the hiring of a building for the depot are confusing. A memo from Owen Ford, a grocer, dated 4 August and given to the Council Chairman, stated that a house had been cleaned and available for nearly a month. A claim was made for rent, even though the house had not been occupied.[6] Owen Ford, with two others, had purchased Lot 47, with a house, on the corner of Jacob and Murray streets in 1855. However, the rent for the depot was increased from 25/- to £2 per month,[7] and was paid to Patrick Kelly, according to the Irish Female Immigrants Details of Expenditure.[8] Presumably Owen Ford had sold his share of the title. Certainly Patrick Kelly, identified as a stockholder in the Lands Title Office archives, owned much land in the area. According to the Gawler Council records of 1858, the earliest available, Kelly owned the property on the corner of Jacob and Murray streets occupied by John Rudall, used as an office and house. This property was very probably the site of the servants depot because later John Rudall was compensated for being kept out of his house for longer than originally arranged. The Gawler Depot opened when the girls arrived, about the second week in August.

The most significant character in the history of the depot was John Reid. He was one of the original settlers who had purchased land available after Colonel Light's Special Gawler Survey. In 1838 Reid's wagon trip from Adelaide to Gawler took three days. He established a successful farm but by 1852, it is claimed, was near ruin as the result of land speculation.[9] He was certainly well known as a local identity. He had financed a German settler, Mr Scheibner, to build the Old Spot Hotel[10] which can still be seen today on the Main North Road, Salisbury Heights. His daughter, Elizabeth, had married a thirty-year-old Irishman, Dr Mahony, in 1849.[11]

John Reid had, with the local Catholic priest, visited the Gawler Depot soon after it was established to find there were thirty-one girls, no bedding and one girl was without blankets! The Matron, Mary Murphy, said she had applied to Mr Moorhouse and he had suggested she use loose straw as bedding. However, she could not find any and was concerned about the risk of fire. John Reid wrote immediately to 'Headquarters' but received no acknowledgement. On his last visit to the depot he saw there were twenty-four girls and still only seven beds. After he had not received any reply to his letter, John Reid wrote to the Colonial Secretary on 21 August about the improper treatment of immigrants. One girl, he reported, was still without blankets. Reid hoped that His Excellency would enquire. Mr Moorhouse, he wrote, 'looks on them as a mere lot of pigs. Straw if to be had is not safe nor is it a fit bed to give them.' Reid reported, with implied criticism, the Chairman of the Mudla Wirra Council had visited only three times in the last fourteen days.[12] The Governor wrote to his Secretary, on the cover note of this letter that he was prepared to sanction any expenditure necessary for the health of the immigrants: 'Each ought to have her own blankets.' Nevertheless the Governor added, 'straw should be put inside backing bought for the purpose and made up by the immigrants.' He also noted that the Chairman was remiss in the exercise of his duty. The reply to John Reid from the Colonial Secretary's office advised that the Governor had sent instructions to the Chairman of the District Council 'who will take steps to remedy the defective arrangements to which you allude'.[13]

During this time Reid, in frustration, rode to Adelaide and 'personally visited' the offices of one of the daily papers to make a statement. The *Adelaide Times* of Saturday 25 August published an article headed 'Irish Female Immigrants – Shameful Neglect', which was scathing about Moorhouse, and immediately opened a public subscription.

> Subscriptions are solicited at the Times and Dispatch Office towards providing beds for the poor Irish female immigrants at Gawler Town, who are left by the Government authorities to sleep on the ground.[14]

By 27 August the paper was reporting that upwards of £12 had been collected. 'Mr Reid had instructed Dr Mahony to provide whatever was necessary without reference to government authorities whose behaviour has been disgraceful.' Reid informed the Colonial Secretary on 28 August that the public 'had contributed a sum sufficient to purchase beds for the girls'.[15] As a result, living conditions in the depot may have been improved somewhat but some girls were still in dire circumstances. Reverend Ryan advised the Female Immigration Board (FIB) on 2 October that thirteen girls were in need of boots and many were in need of bonnets and shawls. The board approved the provision of boots only.[16] Between November and December eight pairs of boots were provided to specifically named girls in the Gawler Depot – M. Degan, M. Hogan, Jane Campbell, Cath Broadrick, Eliza Quinn, Bridget Murray, M. Greenway and Bridget Larkin.

Late in December the FIB dismissed a girl who had refused a placement at Gawler River. The unidentified girl said very definitely that she did not wish to go to the country and was rude to her prospective employer. The girl was advised she could be admitted to the Destitute Asylum because of her insubordination.[17] There are so many similarities between this case and one reported the next month, when names were used, that it is likely it is the same case, despite the discrepancy of dates. Hannah Corrigan's situation was assessed by the board at a meeting in late January. She claimed that she had to leave Mr Gale in the Gawler Ranges because she had to reap in the daytime, milk eleven cows in the evening and do housework. A letter from Mr Gale said he had only four cows, Hannah had stayed only from Friday to Sunday, and he had never asked her to reap, while his wife and daughter always assisted in washing and housework. When the board sent for Hannah to appear, it was found that she had been sent to the Destitute Asylum and the case was dismissed.[18] Another newspaper reported that Mr Gale was from Gawler River, and that Hannah had been admitted to the Destitute Asylum 'owing to an unlooked for event'[19], presumably pregnancy. Perhaps she was anticipating early dismissal from disapproving employers once her condition became obvious.

Mary O'Halloran, recorded on the *Nashwauk* passenger list as aged twenty-five, from Clare, was transported to Gawler in December, either to the depot or directly to a place of employment, whilst in early pregnancy. She was admitted to the Destitute Asylum in May the next year to be confined.[20] No information can be found about her living situation after leaving the wrecked ship. A Henry O'Halloran, also twenty-five, was listed as being one of the persons on the *Nashwauk*, nominated by a Purchaser of Land, E.A. Wright, with £1 deposited by Martin Kelly, although he is not recorded as a passenger. It is very likely that he was Mary's husband, but his whereabouts cannot be established. Perhaps he went to the gold diggings, or had died.

A meeting of Gawler residents, 'an influential assembly', was held in the Old School Room, with W. Duffield in the chair, on Christmas Eve. The closure of the Gawler Depot had been announced in the *Government Gazette* on 13 November. As well, there had been discussion about the Gawler Depot in the Legislative Council on 20 December. It was claimed that the five or six girls at the depot could be 'as well managed in town' without the public expense of maintaining another depot.[21]

Those attending the meeting were angry. 'Had the DC been consulted about the proposed removal of the Immigrants prior to the notice appearing?' asked Dr Nott. It was claimed that 154 girls had been distributed to the Gawler Depot up to 22 December, a quarter of the 600 sent out to all country depots. (In the minutes of evidence of the Select Committee a table records that 129 girls had been sent from the Central Depot to Gawler Town up to 28 January 1856.) Nevertheless, Matron did not have an adequate supply of girls to meet local demand. If the depot was kept open it could provide accommodation for girls travelling further north, thus reducing government expenditure. And where would the girls go who would no longer be required after harvesting? The only reason the Chairman could offer for the closure was the increase of rent, which had gone up to 40/- per week from 25/-.

It was resolved that a group of seven participants at the meeting would draw up a memo to the Governor with a copy to the Legislative Council, proposing that the depot be maintained. The initial recommendation sent in July from the District Council that a permanent depot for both males and females should be established was to be reiterated.[22]

The *Register* reported on 28 December that at the FIB meeting on the previous day nothing was decided about Gawler Town as no official document had come before the board. The Gawler Depot remained open although the FIB had agreed in November that it should be closed from 1 January 1856.[23] Board members felt that the Gawler District could be supplied with servants from the Central Depot. Concern was expressed that country depots were not as well controlled as the Adelaide Depot and Major O'Halloran felt that morals were in 'less danger of corruption' in the city.[24] Not everyone agreed. Richard Tapley later told the Select Committee that the behaviour of country girls was generally much better than of those in town because there were no local establishments of a 'vicious character'.[25]

Gawler Matron Mary Murphy reported to the FIB in January that two girls were sick. One was 'partially insane' as a result of sunstroke, the other was covered with boils from over-exertion while reaping. The board agreed that both were to be sent down to hospital[26] but Matron later advised that only one, E. Dignum, needed to be sent.[27] At a board meeting later in the month there was discussion about the reimbursement of medical costs paid by a settler at Encounter Bay for an Eliza Dignum, suffering sunstroke. It would seem that this Eliza was the E. Dignum from Gawler, who apparently had not recovered properly in the Adelaide Depot's infirmary before she was sent to the Encounter Bay Depot and hired very quickly. Records do not indicate what happened to the other unfortunate lass 'covered with boils'. She may have been Ann Cullen, who was, according to the Register of Cases of Destitution, in March conveyed sick from Gawler to Adelaide.[28] The Gawler Depot had been closed by this time, so it is probable that Ann was dismissed by her employer because she was ill.

In mid January, the board received an answer to its enquiry from Mrs Curtis of Port Gawler. She reported that she had not paid a servant, Ann Lennon, wages of 6/- because she had left without notice and taken goods on false pretences. She said the girl had left claiming 'sore hands' but that that was not the case. After leaving Mrs Curtis she was employed by Mrs Hunter. Ann, who was at the time of the board meeting unemployed and had presumably been temporarily readmitted to the Adelaide Depot, was called in before the board. She said she had not stolen a silver spoon which was found in her box but that it had been placed there in play by children. Her next employer, Mrs Hunter, would give her an excellent character, she said. She had returned to the depot because Mrs Hunter could no longer afford a servant. The board considered her defence reasonable and decided to write to Mrs Hunter for evidence.[29] There is no record, nor newspaper reports, of Mrs Hunter having replied, so presumably Ann found another situation quickly.

Matron Murphy reported to the FIB at the beginning of February that there were only two girls at the Gawler Depot, one on rations and the other supporting herself, presumably with money earned before she was readmitted.[30] The Gawler Depot was closed in early February[31] and transferred to Kapunda.

At its meeting on 13 February the FIB considered a letter from Mr Buttfield complaining about a girl from the Gawler Depot who had left his service. She had been employed at 7/- per week, but was given notice within a week for dirty habits, obscene language and habitual lying. He said she had stayed after dismissal at a public house, where she had been a bride in a marriage ceremony (presumably she had been a bridesmaid!). In a postscript he added that she had gone towards the Kapunda Depot. A note was made in case she applied for readmission.[32]

The legal firm Smith and Cullen rented the property used as the Gawler Depot as an office from 1 January 1856, when the depot was expected to close. At the end of December the FIB had asked the firm for permission to retain the building for another fortnight as there were thirteen girls resident who would have to be removed.[33] It was not until the FIB meeting on 2 February that it was agreed that the house would be vacated that same day and possession given to Smith and Cullen.[34] At a later meeting, the FIB decided that Mr John Rudall, a country partner of the legal firm, be paid £4 per week for five weeks. He had been kept out of the house which he had occupied while it was used as a depot, and had to locate his family to a public house.[35] He was listed as clerk of the Mudla Wirra District Council.[36] There is no recorded evidence that the Rudall family owned any property in the Gawler area at this time either from the rate notices for the Barossa West Council 1855, or the Mudla Wirra Council. No doubt he was relieved the depot was closed so he could shift his family from a local hotel to the property his legal firm was renting from Patrick Kelly.

Crawford's Brewery, Hindmarsh, 1849 (H.H. Glover).
Courtesy of the State Library of South Australia (SLSA: B 7955).

Port Adelaide, 1847 (G.F. Angas).
Courtesy of the State Library of South Australia (SLSA: B15276/7).

Adelaide views: St John's Church, 1845 (F.R. Nixon).
Courtesy of the State Library of South Australia (SLSA: B 52970/7).

Matthew Moorhouse, c. 1870.
Courtesy of the State Library of South Australia (SLSA: B 10848).

George Strickland Kingston, 1838 (S.T. Gill).
Courtesy of the State Library of South Australia (SLSA: B 350).

Rundle Street looking east, 1855 (S.T. Gill).
Courtesy of the State Library of South Australia (SLSA: B 2430).

Wedding photograph of Bridget Riordan (Clare Depot) and Jacob Von Haarsma, at Spring Farm, 1857.
Courtesy of John Tuohy and Denis Connell.

Ormerod Cottages (today), the likely site of the Robe Depot and then a wool store.
Photographer: P. Charles.

Old cottage at Penola (today), typical of the one used for servant girls.
Photographer: P. Charles.

'The Old Spot', 1845 (S. Calvert).
Courtesy of the State Library of South Australia (SLSA: B 9483/8).

Encounter Bay, 1846 (G.F. Angas).
Courtesy of the State Library of South Australia (SLSA: B15276/16).

The Fountain Inn (today), where the Encounter Bay District Council used to meet.
Photographer: P. Charles.

Freeman's Cottage, Mount Barker, 1860 (photograph).
Courtesy of the State Library of South Australia (SLSA: B 3620).

Police station stables (today), close to the site of the Mount Barker Depot.
Photographer: P. Charles.

Kapunda Copper Mine, 1845 (G.F. Angas).
Courtesy of the State Library of South Australia (SLSA: B 7078).

CHAPTER NINE

Encounter Bay: Unsuitable for Service

The original settlers and key personalities of the area were inextricably associated with the servants depots in every country location because the colony was so young and the population so sparse.

Ridgway W. Newland, Congregational Minister, emigrated with his wife and eight children in 1839 on the *Sir Charles Forbes*. He brought with him a party of labourers, including a blacksmith, a stonemason, a shepherd and several ploughmen, and their families. In 1853 Reverend R.W. Newland was appointed first Chairman of the District Council of Encounter Bay, a position he held until his death in 1864.[1] Initially the district boundaries included Waitpinga, Port Elliot and Goolwa, and were not altered until April 1856, not long before the depot was closed. D.M. Mackie was recorded as the clerk.[2] Roads were poor, and river crossings challenging. Even in 1856 the drive from Willunga to Encounter Bay was described as 'certainly a very wretched one'.[3] Transport by ship was preferred. Port Elliot was selected as the port for the River Murray trade, and the railway between Goolwa and Port Elliot was completed in 1854.

At Encounter Bay family relationships were significant in the operation of the depot. Matron Ellen Higgins was married to John Higgins, who was to become the clerk of the newly redefined District Council in 1856. Meetings of the Encounter Bay

District Council were held in the public house at Yilki, the Fountain Inn. John Higgins was also the first deacon of the Tabernacle, the Congregational Chapel built in 1846 by Ridgway Newland. He was clearly a pivotal character in this widely dispersed settlement. The Higgins family was involved with all three key organisations: the depot, the District Council and the Congregational Church. It is recorded that Robert Higgins, the Matron's brother-in-law, an early settler, did the shopping for the servants depot, one imagines not an insignificant task. He was paid for providing beef and food supplies every month until the depot was closed. John Higgins was also reimbursed for provisions from time to time.[4] T.W. Higgins, perhaps another brother to John, became the first Chairman of the District Council of Port Elliot and Goolwa[5] when it was separated from that of Encounter Bay.

The depot at Encounter Bay was specifically constructed for its purpose. In August, expenditure of £370 was approved for the erection of a building under the supervision of Mr Jones[6] for the occupancy of female immigrants. This depot was one of the government buildings on Warland Reserve, by the Hotel Crown, in the area that became known as Victor Harbor. Today there is a plaque erected on the reserve lawn marking the site of the police station; presumably the servants depot was nearby.

The Immigration Agent was informed by Matthew Moorhouse on 7 August that forty single women, who had arrived at Port Adelaide on the *South Sea*, would be transferred to Encounter Bay via the *Yatala*. An additional sixteen would be sent to Yankalilla. Mr Tapley would accompany the girls on board to their destinations.[7] Presumably the building had been completed before the *Yatala* arrived, sometime later that month.

Because no minutes of Female Immigration Board (FIB) meetings are available and members of the press were not allowed to attend sessions until late December 1855, little information about the early operations of the Encounter Bay Depot can be found. It is impossible to provide accurate figures about the number of occupants during the first few months. Early in October Moorhouse advised the Immigration Agent that the steamer *Melbourne* would take thirty Irish female immigrants to Encounter Bay. It was subsequently recorded that twenty female immigrants were conveyed to Encounter Bay via the *Melbourne* on 12 October.[8] Yet at the Encounter Bay District Council meeting on 20 October it was noted that thirty-one had arrived and that some disturbance had occurred.[9] There can be no doubt that at least twenty girls were sent!

At the Encounter Bay District Council meeting on 3 November, the Chairman reported instances of insubordination by several inmates of the depot. It was agreed that rioters would be suppressed by expulsion 'if needful'.[10] As council meetings were usually attended by the Chairman with the Clerk and one other councillor, power was exercised by very few, but a month later at the next meeting the Chairman reported that order had been restored.[11] There had been no expulsions and there are no other references to the depot in the council minutes for that year.

A press report early in January of an FIB meeting in Adelaide illustrated some of the dilemmas presented to Matron Higgins as well as to board members. The FIB considered an application for readmission to the Adelaide Depot from Mary Reagan. She had returned to the Central Depot from Encounter Bay because she had been there so long, unemployed since early December. Mary had an 'excellent character' report from Matron, and a letter, and hoped that she would be readmitted. Father Ryan, it was reported, had admitted her to the Central Depot temporarily until the meeting. Such kindness in providing accommodation for a servant pending a board hearing was in direct contravention of official policy. Mary told the board she had paid her own fare by mail coach from

Encounter Bay with money she had brought with her to the colony. She had a friend in service in Adelaide. On this occasion Governor MacDonnell's views that girls shouldn't be readmitted prevailed. Despite her initiative and good references Mary was refused readmission.[12] The board hoped that her friend could help her to find accommodation until she found work.

Dr MacIntyre was paid for attending five girls at the Encounter Bay Depot between November and December. At an FIB meeting on 26 January 1856 he reported that Maria Campbell was dangerously ill[13] and he was sending her to Adelaide.[14] A fare was paid for her to travel by steamer from Port Elliot.[15] Unfortunately there is no further record of Maria.

Surprisingly, the issue of employee job security, not a common concern in the young nineteenth-century colony, was raised at this depot. At an FIB meeting in January, a letter was read out from Reverend John Watson, the first incumbent Anglican priest appointed to Port Elliot. He was quite happy to employ a girl he had selected from the depot but not when a contract of employment for six months was the condition of hire. Another settler had also objected to this new condition of employment. He questioned the legality of the requirement and asked the board to reconsider.[16] The board replied that no such regulation existed and Moorhouse was directed to publish the letter and to write to Matron Higgins for an explanation. It was Newland who provided the requested explanation, not Mrs Higgins. He reminded the board that his first instruction had been on no account to permit readmission. However there were difficulties. He found that girls were often returned to the depot after two or three weeks on some pretext or other, and when he would visit he very seldom could find good reason. The employers were people with little or no education and not accustomed to employing servants, so he had introduced a minimum period of hire. 'I may have overstepped boundaries of my authority, but Mrs Higgins will say the regulations have had good effect although unenforceable.'[17] The board ordered that this reply should be made public and a copy sent to Reverend Watson. Watson's response was considered by the board on 23 January, but unfortunately was not released. 'We refrain from publishing it as it is no longer of importance to the public – as attack and reply have done justice to both parties.'[18] It seems that although Reverend Newland's ideas were unacceptable to some potential employers they were viewed sympathetically by members of the board.

Responsibility for health care was another contentious issue raised at Encounter Bay. A letter was read at a board meeting from an employer at Lyndoch Valley. Mr Hipwell had, with some difficulty and considerable expense, provided medical attention to Eliza Dignum who had only been a week in service. She had suffered sunstroke due, he felt, to her own lack of caution, and he was seeking to recover his costs. Major O'Halloran argued that if the board rejected Mr Hipwell's application, settlers would be deterred from acting with the same prompt and hearty humanity in future.[19] The FIB deliberated over this matter for some time, but despite O'Halloran's views, eventually refused to pay.[20] It is reasonable to assume that Eliza was the E. Dignum sent from Gawler to the Adelaide Depot Infirmary suffering sunstroke earlier in the month. It is probable that she had not fully recovered before she was sent on to Encounter Bay and that she had worked diligently to please her new employer and over-exerted herself.

The FIB was advised of the unauthorised departure from the Encounter Bay Depot of Catherine Quinlam, so that she would be refused readmission to the Adelaide Depot. Late in January Catherine presented at the gates of the Central Depot and was called before the board. It appeared to the reporter that she had hoped to stay at the depot whilst she found a way to go to friends at Kapunda.[21] The *Adelaide Times*[22] reported that a

Catherine Quinley told the FIB she had left the Encounter Bay Depot because her clothes were wearing out. However, there was evidence, from a letter found in her possession, that she had intended to stop in Adelaide until she had the means to go to Kapunda (a search of an applicant's belongings was apparently considered acceptable). Catherine was refused readmission.

There was constant controversy about supply and demand for servant labour in the Encounter Bay region during the next few months. Early in February it was reported to the FIB that two girls had been expelled for refusing fair wages.[23] It seems that some girls sent to Encounter Bay were not willing to conform to what they considered unreasonable expectations. The FIB refused to send more girls, as Matron Higgins requested, until the eight remaining had been hired.[24] A week later this decision was repeated. On 16 February the board agreed to meet only once a week, so it wasn't until 23 February that Matron's explanation for her request was tabled. She reported that in the previous week there were six girls in the depot. Two were sick and the remaining four could not milk and were 'entirely unfit' for country work.[25] Matron said that if twenty more were sent, and appropriate, they could be found situations. Board member Michael Ryan was dubious, and suspected that Matron just wanted to keep the depot open. Eighty girls had already been sent, he claimed (although by the end of January 1856, ninety-one girls had been sent from the Central Depot according to the Select Committee minutes of evidence), and he thought 'not many more would be required'. It was agreed to seek independent advice from Reverend Newland.[26]

The reply from Newland indicated that twenty girls could be placed within two months if skilled in country work. Otherwise placement might take up to three months. He objected to the insinuation about Matron Higgins's motives. She was financially independent and came from a very respectable situation. She had two or three cows, taught the girls to milk, make bread, and cook. Nevertheless, Father Ryan was still suspicious and after some discussion the board decided to send ten girls only. Patrick Ennis, the Yard Supervisor, was called into the meeting and said there were not ten girls suited for country work available currently in the Central Depot. Consequently the board ordered a fresh classification be made so that any girl who refused to take a situation she had said she was 'fit for' would be dismissed.[27]

To further complicate the board's assessment of the potential work placements Moorhouse reported that he had spoken to the Governor, who had ridden through the neighbouring countryside early in March and thought it was well supplied.[28]

By the end of that month it was reported that nine girls had been employed, some with comparatively high wages; two for 7/- and two for 6/-.[29]

At a meeting in mid April, it was noted that four girls had been sent and the two who could milk were hired immediately. Amazingly, given the board's repeated refusal over the previous two months to send more, it was agreed that twenty girls be supplied – probably because the board was shortly to disband. The girls were not to go all at once, but a few at a time.[30]

Two weeks after the board's final meeting, Matthew Moorhouse, the former Superintendent, recommended the closure of the Encounter Bay Depot, where there were four remaining residents. Three caused some concern. In a letter to Moorhouse, Matron Higgins wrote that she was sorry to report that Bridget Cahill (or Cahile), the only girl who could milk, had been returned twice. She was 'so delicate that, through no fault of hers, she was unable to do servant's duties'.[31] There was also difficulty with two other girls, Rosa and Jane McGurk, who were to return to the Adelaide Depot on board the *Melbourne*. Moorhouse, no longer with an FIB to advise him, had written to the Colonial Secretary asking for 'instructions about how to act with these girls should they arrive'.[32] A comment on the front cover of this memo, initialled by Governor MacDonnell and dated 23 May read: 'he ought not to receive into the depot the two girls in question.' The Colonial Secretary subsequently formally wrote to Moorhouse with this advice. Unfortunately there is no information available which would explain this decision. Had the McGurks behaved inappropriately? Was one ill and being nursed by the other? Perhaps they were simply 'unsuitable for service'. Presumably they were returned to Adelaide and somehow found accommodation and work.

CHAPTER TEN

Mount Barker: Tragedy

From very early in the life of the colony the Mount Barker District was reputed to provide excellent grazing land. Squatters used the pasture for the sheep and cattle brought overland from interstate. The first special survey in the colony was purchased in 1839.

> … the sum of $4,000 was paid in to the hands of the Colonial Treasurer (Osmond Gilles Esq) … for the priority of choice of an equal number of acres out of 15,000 to be surveyed in the beautiful and fertile district of Mount Barker.[1]

Large tracts of land were purchased under the Special Survey Provisions, by a consortium of investors from New South Wales, the South Australian Company, and others. The partners of this first Special Survey in Mount Barker, William Hampden Dutton, Duncan McFarlane and John Finnis, announced in February 1840 they would lay out a township at Mount Barker using half-acre allotments, with reserves for churches and schools.[2]

The town became the service centre for a thriving farming district. John Dunn and his son, using locally quarried stone, constructed their steam flour mill, which became the town's key asset. Father Michael O'Brien was appointed in 1848 to the Mount Barker Catholic Mission, a widely dispersed area including Crafers, Wellington and Mount Torrens, and remained for fourteen years. The Church of St Francis de Sale was consecrated by Bishop Murphy in 1851,[3] on the site of the current school. The Methodists, in the same year, opened their church made of stone which John Dunn helped quarry. Dunn in his memoirs, *A Miller's Tale*, reported the 1855 arrival of Reverend Flockart, 'the first married Wesleyan minister'.[4] There are many indicators that the town rapidly increased in size. In 1851 a visitor estimated the population to be about 250, with sixty tenements.[5] By 1855 there were several schools in the town, the Great Eastern Road provided reasonable access with a toll no longer levied, and there was a regular mail service. There were flourishing fruit and vegetable gardens, two hotels, a local court house, a post office and a police barracks.

The first District Council was established in 1853. The minutes of each fortnightly meeting reveal that roads and rates were predominant concerns.[6] The Mount Barker Female Immigration Depot (FID) was mentioned twice in 1855 and not at all the next year! On the first of these occasions it was noted that council agreed on 9 July, after reading Governor MacDonnell's circular, that twenty-five servant girls could be immediately accommodated. A good deal of community consultation must then have transpired. As a result the local Magistrate, Francis Davison, replied on behalf of five councils, including Nairne and Onkaparinga, that there was a wish to cooperate. The councils of Echunga and Macclesfield, having no suitable building, would use Mount Barker as a base.[7] There were offers to provide accommodation for a depot in large family properties at Woodside, Balhannah and Mount Barker. However, all offers of rental properties and supervision were declined, for reasons not at all clear. The depot was eventually established in Hutchinson Street, close to the police barracks, very probably close to the old stone stables in Gawler Street. The property was hired from R.B. Andrews at an annual rental of £52. Mr Andrews was clerk of the District Council according to the *South Australian Almanack and General Directory, 1855*. Records show that rental was paid from September[8] and, although there are no earlier financial records available, it is probable the depot was established about that time.

There was some opposition to the establishment of a depot. Robert Davenport from Macclesfield felt that there was a 'lesser demand for servants on account of the general poverty of the season and scarcity of food'. English and Scottish servants 'are preferred to the ignorant and coarse class sent from Ireland'.[9]

Matron Eliza Frankpitt was paid the standard £4-10-0 per month. She had been a nurse at the Destitute Asylum prior to taking up her position.[10] She was described by Matron Ross, who had been at the Adelaide Depot for several years, as a very clever, active woman, who ran a successful depot.[11] John B. Shepherdson, the first Director of Schools in South Australia, was appointed Clerk of the Local Court in 1850.[12] In 1855 he was elected Chairman of the District Council. Shepherdson signed all correspondence about the depot even after Benjamin Gray was elected Chairman in 1856,[13] perhaps indicating that he maintained a personal interest in its operation. In 1856 he was appointed Deputy Registrar for Births, Deaths and Marriages in Mount Barker.[14]

The *Register* reported in November 1855 that seventy-one girls had been sent, and forty-eight engaged by 26 October. Since then twelve more had been sent and more requested. By 8 November the total number sent from the Central Depot was eighty-three. Sixty-seven had gone and sixteen remained. Much credit was due to Matron Frankpitt and her husband.[15]

Shepherdson informed his fellow councillors in December that some of the girls were refusing to take good positions because they were required to 'tender temporary assistance in the field during the busy seasons of hay making and harvest'. When the Female Immigration Board (FIB) supported these refractory girls the Chairman considered the decision was 'calculated to promote insubordination highly prejudicial to the interest of the establishment'. Council unanimously agreed that girls refusing employment should not be maintained at government expense. The minutes record that Governor MacDonnell 'during his visit a few days ago' directed the Matron to expel girls who refused to take any offer of employment.[16] He thus created a dilemma for the board. If girls should take temporary work should they not then be readmitted when their employment ceased? This issue remained a cause of conflict between the Governor and the FIB, and not only at the Mount Barker Depot.

William Rundle was paid 10/- per person for transporting girls from Adelaide to Mount Barker by bullock dray.[17] There also must have been other conveyances because Mrs Frankpitt reported a disastrous accident at Christmas time. The cart bringing a 'Scotch family of five sisters', sent out by the board, had overturned near Mount Barker, and the girls were thrown out. The driver was leading his horses at the time. Three girls suffered slight bruising. Another whose leg had broken in three places was taken to a neighbouring cottage and attended by Dr Walker.[18] The girl's mother was in the Destitute Asylum and Moorhouse directed, immediately, that she be sent up to her daughter.[19] This was an act of considerable generosity for that time, by a very busy administrator. Government archives record that an Ann Morrison had her leg amputated; that a cottage was rented for her for three weeks and that two doctors attended the amputation. Sadly she died and was buried in January. Despite the local upheaval caused by this accident, the FIB, on receipt of a letter from the District Council outlining costs, was exceptionally parsimonious. The cottage hired for Ann Morrison was considered too expensive, as there were cheaper ones available and as good. Similarly the coffin used for her burial was considered too expensive and should have been the kind provided for paupers.[20] Medical costs were, however, considered appropriate![21]

It seems that either Matron Frankpitt or the newspaper journalist became confused about the names of the accident victims, or perhaps there were more passengers on the dray than reported. At the board meeting on the 16 February, it was reported that Matron had sent back one of the 'Scotch girls' who had been hurt, as her foot was still very weak.[22] There is much confusion about the name of this accident victim. The Mary Loray who suffered contusions from the dray accident, according to one record[23], was very probably the Mary Lolpey who, 'upset from Rundle's dray', was sent to the Central Depot.[24] In addition, Dr Walker is recorded as having attended Mary Lorpey six times.[25]

Margaret Fitzgerald, who just possibly may have been the Margaret Fitzgerald listed as a passenger on the *Nashwauk*, had also been attended by Dr Walker in January. She required pills and lotions, but it is not clear whether or not she was an accident victim.[26] Records show that the Margaret Fitzgerald from the *Nashwauk* had, in August 1855, been engaged from the Clare Depot for six months by Mr Diarwood of Armagh. It is possible that she was not required for that period, or had become ill and had been returned to the Adelaide Depot, and sent from there to Mount Barker. However it is much more likely that there were two girls named Margaret Fitzgerald who arrived in 1855.

January was a month of much activity at Mount Barker, perhaps because the Willunga Depot was closed. At the first meeting in the new year Matron Frankpitt reported twenty-four girls had been employed during the last week, most at 4/- per week and six at 5/-.[27] At the FIB meeting on 9 January, at the time that the Governor and the board were in conflict about a policy of no readmission, Matron reported that there were sixteen girls in the depot who could have got temporary outdoor work if they had consented, and so risked not being readmitted. Members of the board were not concerned about these refusals, acknowledging the dilemma facing the girls. Major Thomas O'Halloran provided an excuse by saying that the girls would do harvest work if paid properly; and Michael Ryan agreed.[28] Matron then requested ten more girls for home service and reported that the last girls sent were 'quite unfit'.[29] A few days later she reported that twenty-two girls had been employed, none for less than two months.[30]

Sadly, employment with a responsible settler did not always ensure a stable future life. William Gosse, the Medical Officer responsible for the Adelaide Depot, reported to the Select Committee of Enquiry that one girl had been brought from Mount Barker 'some time ago, whose care required more caution than had been exercised ... she was in a high state of fever and died that night'. The master had brought in the girl himself. 'She had been out of her mind two or three days and in charge of police as a lunatic.'[31]

The Mount Barker Depot presented the board with some discomfort. A letter of complaint was received by the FIB from Mr Barrett of Langhorne Creek, which illustrates some of the practical difficulties experienced by depot administrators. Mr Barrett had gone to the Mount Barker Depot, selected and hired a girl and booked a place for her on the mail coach. However, he was sent a different girl. Matron explained that Mr Barrett had not removed the girl he had chosen immediately and so the girl had then accepted another more 'eligible' offer, against Matron's advice. Matron had therefore sent the 'next best girl' to Mr Barrett. She was prepared to pay this girl's fare back to the depot if she was not acceptable to him. In future Matron would insist that employers must remove girls at the time of hiring.[32]

At the same meeting that the board was told that Ann Morrison (the girl whose leg was amputated after the accident) had been buried, Matron also reported that one girl, Catherine Egan, had left her situation on the advice of the local missionary, Father Michael O'Brien. 'She had been interfered with in her religion.' Presumably she was not permitted to attend Catholic church services. The board was not impressed and felt that O'Brien should have remonstrated with the girl's employer. Fortunately, Catherine had gone immediately to 'another master'.

Girls from the Mount Barker Depot were certainly not all malleable. Mary Riley had run away from her situation and had come to Adelaide against Matron's advice,[33] because she had a sister in Adelaide and an aunt in Melbourne. She had 'applied at the gate' of the Adelaide Depot and was refused readmission to any depot.[34] This could not have been the Mary Riley (Byall?), a passenger on the *Nashwauk* – who told the Legislative Council Select Committee she had originally applied to go to Sydney, had never been in service, and had been ill for her first five months in the colony. Another girl, Mary McCaddell had left her place, Matron reported, 'without reason' and was also refused readmission.

Late in January, William Giles complained to the FIB that Margaret Donady, who was paid 5/- per week, refused to get up early to wash and 'had decamped without notice' and gone to town. She must have applied for readmission because she was called before the board and it was agreed that she was to be refused readmission not only to the Central Depot but to any other depot.[35]

It was noted at the FIB meeting on 23 February 1856 that there were seventeen girls in the depot in the previous week.[36] It was agreed at this meeting that names of both servants and employers would be withheld from publication.

At the Select Committee hearing in February Matron Ross said that about 200 had been employed from the Mount Barker Depot.[37] Figures provided to the Select Committee show that

241 girls had been sent there from the Central Depot by the end of January 1856, so approximately forty had either been not engaged or had been returned. There were some unexpected reasons. At the first FIB meeting in March, a letter was read from Matron Frankpitt in which she reported that four girls had been hired. However, her main concern was the issue of readmission. The name was noted of one girl, who had left her situation at Lobethal one week early despite an offer of increased wages, so that she would not be readmitted. Similarly the names of several girls who had left apparently good situations 'simply to go to Adelaide because they had grown tired of the country' were recorded to ensure that they would be refused readmission at the Central Depot.

It was at this March meeting that two girls from Mount Barker were assessed for readmission to the Adelaide Depot, producing 'discharges and good characters from their place'. Mrs Frankpitt had refused to readmit them so they had come to town. Apparently because of their good references, the girls were readmitted and the board ordered Moorhouse to write to Matron directing her not to refuse readmission for good cases.[38] At the next board meeting Matron Frankpitt's explanation was read. One of these girls had left her situation without sufficient reason and the other was too ill. Consequently one was dismissed from the Central Depot and the other given medical attention, reported the *Adelaide Times*.[39] The *Register* provided more details of Matron's explanations. The girl she refused to readmit had run away to Adelaide when the Mount Barker Depot was first established. She had returned to the depot after leaving a position at Green Town, falsely saying she had been sent away. She had refused two or three other positions until Mr Shepherson had threatened to dismiss her. She was only fit for outside work and another readmission would provide a bad example to the other girls.[40] Had she forged her discharge notice or did Matron find her repeated readmissions intolerable?

Moorhouse reported to the board early in March that the Governor had ridden through the country. It seemed to him to be well supplied and he thought there was not want of servants.[41] Nevertheless the FIB continued to supply girls for whom positions were found.

Matron Frankpitt's strong views about behaviour led to a heated argument between Michael Ryan and Major O'Halloran at an FIB meeting at the end of the month. Matron Frankpitt had dismissed a girl because of her 'insolent conduct', although she had been discharged with good character from her last mistress. Matron claimed the girl had called her a liar three times. As a result of her dismissal the aggrieved girl had travelled to the city at her own expense to seek readmission at the Cental Depot and was subsequently called before the board. She said that Matron Frankpitt had provoked her by asserting that a man, who was whistling outside, was doing so as a signal to her, which was not true and very unfair as she did not know the man and had never spoken to him. There were seventeen other girls with her in the depot and she was getting into bed at the time. Father Ryan was supportive of the girl and considered the action of the Matron unjustifiable. O'Halloran remarked that they had only the girl's statement against the well-known good character of Mrs Frankpitt. He would readmit with reprimand, whereas Father Ryan would not reprimand without further enquiry. George Kingston pointed out that the girl was the same one who in February had been readmitted to the Adelaide Depot from the London Coffee House after reporting that it was a house of ill-fame. The *Adelaide Times*, when reporting that allegation, had named the girl as Jane Callilay. Kingston, recalling the Coffee House incident, said that if Jane had been 'quite proper she should have left immediately' and not stayed for several days after she was aware of its disgraceful character. Obviously, in his opinion, loss of wages was not a consideration. O'Halloran suggested that the girl's statement should be submitted to Mrs Frankpitt and the girl readmitted conditionally.[42] J.B. Shepherdson wrote the report for the next meeting as Mrs Frankpitt's husband had just died. He could not substantiate the case against Jane Callilay but the board nevertheless agreed upon a reprimand as an example to others, only to find that she had been hired out during the week!

The board read a letter from a Mrs Freeman who complained that she had been refused a servant because she and her husband were 'commonly reputed drunkards'. A gentleman who was 'casually present' said that the Freemans were highly respected. The board was of the general opinion that Matron Frankpitt was justified in refusing to send a girl to a house of reputed drunkards and noted at the same time that Matron had no power to prevent any girl hiring herself. The letter was sent to Mrs Frankpitt for her reply. Shepherdson, replying for her, was so ambiguous about the claim that the Freemans were drunkards that the board felt unable to make any decision.[43]

At the same meeting, at the end of March, it was reported that nine of the twelve girls sent during the week had been hired, two at 7/-, two at 6/- and three at 3/-. There were nine girls in the depot and one sick.[44]

Matron Frankpitt was well able to defend her girls from exploitation. She reported to the board that she had summonsed a man and recovered a month's wages.[45] Michael Kelly, an Irish immigrant settler, was charged with refusing to pay wages and unfair dismissal of Bridget Tore in the Magistrates Court on 18 January 1856. He was found guilty and directed to repay and re-employ Bridget. In another case, in March, Moses Hillier was found guilty of refusing to pay some balance of wages to Ellen Murphy.[46]

The number of marriages registered at the Mount Barker Catholic Mission increased dramatically after the establishment of the depot, reflecting the impact of the many Irish Catholic female immigrants. Whereas in 1852–1855 there were twenty-five marriages recorded, in 1856–1859 there were seventy-three. Similarly, the number of baptisms rose. In 1855 there were fifty-two and two years later there were seventy-six.[47]

One marriage recorded in the Catholic Archives may have been that of a *Nashwauk* passenger. Mary Ryan married John O'Connor in November 1857. The Mary Ryan from the ship, who was aged twenty on the passenger list but twenty-two when recorded in the Cases of Destitution, was living at the Stagg Inn in Rundle Street in July 1855 when recommended for relief. She had lost her position due to inefficiency. Maybe this Mary was unable to find work, was admitted to the Adelaide Depot and was then transferred to the Mount Barker Depot.

At the second to last FIB meeting it was reported that nine girls had been hired. There are no other records of activities at the depot, and presumably it closed not long after the board disbanded at the end of April. Matron Frankpitt's expenses for returning to Adelaide were paid in November 1856,[48] several months after the depot had been closed. The records of *Expenditure at Adelaide and Country depots, 1855–1856*, indicate that payments were often late. Perhaps Mrs Frankpitt and her family remained with friends in Mount Barker whilst preparing to return to the city.

It is not possible accurately to report the total number of girls sent to Mount Barker over the entire period of operation. However, statistics presented to the last FIB meeting indicated that 238 girls had left the depot for service. There can be no doubt that Mount Barker Depot was the largest and the most successful country depot.

CHAPTER ELEVEN

Kapunda: The Last Chance

The County of Light was proclaimed in 1842 and the Hundred of Kapunda not until 1851. The town of North Kapunda was laid out by the trustees of the North Kapunda Mining Company and by 1851 there were three churches: Catholic, Wesleyan and Bible Christian. An indenture in the Lands Title Office archives indicates that Mr Abrahams bought three town sections (each of eighty acres) from the North Kapunda Mining Company between 1854 and 1856. He was clearly a significant local landowner. By 1861 the census lists 397 stone buildings, forty wooden houses and fifteen tents in the town. The bridge over the River Light was not built until 1856. The township was bereft of timber, had roads which were either mud or dust depending on the season, and was enveloped with smoke and fumes from the mine.[1] It was chosen as a location for a Female Immigration Depot (FID) because it was between Gawler and Clare.

Many Irish labourers arriving to work at the mines put up huts at nearby Baker's Flat.[2] Nearly all were Catholic. The first religious service in the area, held by Father Michael Ryan during one of his early missionary tours, was reputed to be at the mines in 1845. Father Fallon was the resident Catholic priest in 1849 and a new church was built in 1854,[3] when there was a significant increase in the number of Irish labourers.

For a servants depot Mr Abrahams offered premises in Baker Street known as the Murray Company's Store for £50 for six months, commencing Monday, 2 February 1856.[4] He had attended a Female Immigration Board (FIB) meeting on 30 January to negotiate the lease.[5] The depot stood near the site of the original Miners Arms Hotel, and was later used for Anglican then Baptist church services.[6]

According to the Select Committee report, the Gawler Depot was transferred to Kapunda on 8 February 1856. The *Adelaide Times* reported that Matron Mary Murphy, with one girl, luggage and utensils, was moved from Gawler to Kapunda, by Haines & Co.[7] In addition Haines & Co. were paid for conveying four girls, with boxes and cooking utensils from Clare.[8]

Matron Murphy had requested the name of someone in authority to whom she was responsible. The local medical practitioner, Dr Blood, was appointed Comptroller,[9] and it was recorded at a later meeting that he agreed to give Matron the benefit of his advice and experience![10] Beds from the Clare Depot, if considered worth moving, were to be sent to Kapunda.[11] Matron reported her arrival to the FIB and requested more girls.[12] Eleven arrived shortly after and at the next FIB meeting it was noted that twenty girls were now at the Kapunda Depot. Each day three girls, and their boxes, were despatched from the Central Depot until thirty had been sent.[13] Haines & Co. were paid for removing forty-eight girls from Adelaide in February and March and it is not at all clear whether the forty-eight included the initial eleven or whether a total of fifty-nine girls were transported to the depot. Twenty-two more were conveyed from March to May and two in June.[14]

At the first FIB meeting in March the board noted that Matron Murphy, on the advice of Dr Blood, who was to become Kapunda's first Mayor, had expelled a 'badly conducted' girl.[15] No other information was offered and the board agreed that more details should have been provided. Thirteen girls had been hired and thirteen remained.[16]

A letter from Mr Rogers claiming medical and funeral

expenses for Mary Tierney, whom he had hired from a depot, was considered by the board in April. The board noted that it was his second claim for reimbursement. There is no death registered but early in January a coffin was bought and a grave dug at Kapunda for Mary Tierney who had died after being in Mr Roger's employment.[17] Presumably Mary had been hired from the Clare Depot, prior to the establishment of the Kapunda facility.

At an FIB meeting in mid February, a girl, apparently a resident at the Adelaide Depot, was charged with refusing a situation at Burra for 3/- per week. She said she was too ill to do washing and ironing. O'Halloran recommended that she be sent to Kapunda or be dismissed. An elderly woman, who was her aunt, appeared before the board and got permission to go with her niece.[18] At the end of March, Matron reported to the FIB that the aunt, a Mrs Isaacs, who had been a ship's Matron, was very troublesome. She had left for Adelaide with her niece after 'national animosities'.[19] Presumably both were evicted.

Early in April there were twenty-four in the depot and at the FIB meeting a few weeks later it was noted that seventeen girls remained.[20] During the month another girl was expelled, this time for misconduct, having left the depot without permission and staying away overnight.[21]

Statistics provided early in May 1856 indicate that sixty girls had left Kapunda for service.[22]

Moorhouse, as former Superintendent, wrote on 24 July: 'Judging from Matron's returns I consider the neighbourhood must be pretty well supplied, no girl having been hired from the 4th–18th July.' Eight girls remained.[23] Nevertheless, by the time the depot was closed on 14 August only one girl and cooking utensils were returned to Adelaide.[23]

The last country depot was closed and the Adelaide Depot had been considerably reduced. Servant girls were having no difficulty finding work by mid 1856.

CHAPTER TWELVE

The Adelaide Depot

Living Conditions

What sort of a home, albeit temporary, did the Central Depot provide for newcomers, compared to the country depots? No doubt attempts were made to help inmates adjust to a very different climate and to living in a large institution. Continuous efforts were made to enlarge buildings and to provide clean and practical facilities, both before and after the disturbance caused by Moorhouse assaulting a servant girl. Probably many girls were comforted by the large number of others in the same situation in the depot and by contact with friends. For many the facilities were much better than those in their homes in Ireland. Matron Ross reported that there used to be a great deal of dancing in the evenings.[1]

The Governor approved the building of a bake house in July 1855.[2] This was to supply the Female Immigration Depot (FID), the Destitute Asylum and the Lunatic Asylum,[3] as well as the gaol and the hospital.[4] It wasn't until January 1856 that Moorhouse requested approval from the Female Immigration Board (FIB) for the employment of a baker. 'His Excellency appears very desirous of trying the experiment of baking.'[5] There were ovens which could provide for a thousand people.[6] The baker would only require two women to help.[7] At an FIB meeting on 26 January two newly baked loaves were submitted and approved.[8] By March it was reported that the bake house experiment seemed to be a *fait accompli*.[9] It was not until August that Moorhouse requested the transfer of the baker's wages to the Destitute Poor Department,[10] as the FID was closing. The bakery had provided employment for a few of the occupants of the FID. Matron Ross told the Select Committee that some girls 'assist the baker', although the baker only required two girls at any one time.

Misconduct in the Adelaide Depot

Any large group of displaced, unattached young women, with uncertain futures, in an unfamiliar environment, would include, inevitably, some recalcitrant individuals. A few of the Irish girls exhibited unacceptable behaviour which then sullied the good name of their compatriots.

In December a newspaper article appeared headed 'Moral State of the Depot'. A police report stated that a young woman was fined 5/- for being drunk on North Terrace. She came from Clare in Ireland, had been in the depot for two months, and had no situation. She said she had no money but when told that the alternative to non-payment was imprisonment, she quickly produced 5/-. The newspaper article commented on the anomalous situation where girls were able to earn while being supported at public expense. 'Young women in Adelaide may be frequently seen selling various kinds of female work executed at the depot.' An inquiry was suggested.[11] Two days later the editor of the *Register* expressed a 'hope that the investigation now being conducted will be thoroughly carried out'. Mr Baker in the Legislative Council reported that he often passed the Parklands Depot and could speak to the misconduct of its inmates.[12]

The board was well aware of this public disreputable behaviour and early in December had considered three options. One was solitary confinement, which board members recognised as illegal. The second was the reduction of rations, both in quality and quantity, which could lead to inmates being undernourished. The third was a work test, which members considered impracticable. The board, therefore, recommended that His Excellency approve the closing of the outer gates so that the girls would require special permission to go out. The Governor approved:

> as the Board seems to wish further powers of punishing the refractory girls I'm quite prepared, with the advice of my Council, to introduce a legislative measure based on recommendations of the Board to invest them with all necessary powers.[13]

He also suggested that further inquiries be made into the option of a labour test.[14] Meanwhile, a sentry box was created and a gatekeeper was appointed from 18 December at a salary of £1 per week and rations.[15] At this time girls employed from depots were fortunate if they were paid half the gatekeeper's salary. A police constable was placed on duty from sundown till 6 am on Sundays and all public holidays. A gatekeeper would be on duty from 8 am till sunset.[16]

Clearly the press had some impact on early colonial administration. It was at the next meeting of the FIB on the 27 December that a reporter was allowed in for the first time. The establishment of a gatekeeper, the new rules about visitors and the girls not being allowed to go out from the depot without permission were duly reported.[17] In answer to a question in the Legislative Council, Mr Baker was reassured by the Colonial Secretary that the females were now kept within the walls.[18]

Not surprisingly, conditions in the depot seemed much like those of a boarding school; there were harsh penalties for those who broke the rules. Just after new year's eve, which the girls had attempted to celebrate in their wards, a girl was brought before the FIB for being very impertinent to Matron Ross. Mrs William Ross had been Matron to the Irish orphans in 1850 prior to being appointed to the depot so was very experienced. The girl was reported because of her comments about the new year festivities. 'It's an innocent amusement. Let's hear no more about it,' she had said. She was severely reprimanded.[19] Clearly residents should not express opinions to their supervisors.

At the end of January two girls were 'turned out' for refusing to scrub floors as requested by Matron Ross. Four girls were reprimanded for laughing and otherwise 'disturbing the general repose after the hours of ringing the bell'.[20] Ann McEvoy and Sarah Keogh were brought before the board for quarrelling and creating a disturbance. The *Register* reported that one quarrel was so violent that the police were called in. Ann McEvoy had 'taken a knife' to Matron and was dismissed, and Sarah was reprimanded.[21]

Sarah Keogh was a witness to the Select Committee Enquiry and her evidence illustrates the dismal experiences which probably contributed to her unacceptable behaviour. She was a dressmaker who had never been in service at home and had been in the depot for eight months. She said she had worked at Gawler Town for a family of nine, where she cooked, washed, milked one cow, and collected and cut up wood. She had sore eyes and her master had said she was not capable after two weeks. She had gone to Encounter Bay but had been sent back as unfit for country work.[22] Undoubtedly employment prospects for dressmakers were bleak.

Ellen Dixon, who had been 'rather insolent and abusive' to Mr Ennis, the Yard Supervisor, was dismissed but, due to his intercession, was permitted a lapse of one week to give her a chance of finding employment.[23]

Occupation

What did the girls do in the depot? During the long ship voyage they had the opportunity of going to school and/or making clothes. Matron Ross, who said she had been a Matron for four years[24], explained that there was no daily occupation, but that the girls busied themselves with needlework and knitting. She said that a great number had come from manufactories where needlework and embroidery was made.[25] A journalist inspecting the depot at the end of the year commented approvingly that the girls were sitting on their boxes in their dormitories, engaged in needlework, knitting or reading.[26] A committee of ladies provided cotton which enabled girls to manufacture articles of needlework and embroidery for sale. The girls kept the proceeds.

John Baker had asked a question in the Legislative Council prior to Christmas about whether girls in the depot were earning money from day work and returning at night to be rationed at public expense. The answer provided indicated that 'hitherto the immigrants had not been prevented, whilst drawing their support from government, from occupying any portion of their time for hire work without giving any account of the same'.[27] The impact of this political scrutiny on the board's decisions was unfortunate. In January a girl in the depot was refused permission to go out and wash for two or three days a week because the board did not want girls to reside in the depot at government expense and make money for themselves.[28] 'The Depot would become a lodging house.'[29] Nevertheless, there were clearly differing opinions among board members which resulted in ambiguous, at times contradictory, decisions.

At an FIB meeting later in January Major O'Halloran thought it desirable to obtain needlework for the girls. He suggested that girls could be employed in 'linen work' for the hospital but Chairman G.S. Kingston objected because he thought such activity would interfere with employment prospects.[30] Approximately six weeks later Dr Gosse requested that the girls make linen goods, twenty-four shirts and chemises and other articles for the hospital. Reverend Ryan was sure that plenty of girls would volunteer without expecting payment and this time the board ordered the job to be done.[31] Unpaid employment, it seems, was not a contentious issue for board members and so Dr Gosse's request was accepted.

Patrick Ennis, Yard Supervisor, told the Select Committee that some residents had been employed making sacks for Messrs Dutton & McDermott. This work was usually given to girls in need of boots.[32] An offer from Thomas Cain of machinery to be used for making Scotch tweed, including a carding machine, was rejected by the board in February. No reason was given.[33] A letter from Oliver Richardson, Acting Colonial Secretary, advised that the board 'was not in a position at present to recommend the acceptance of Mr Cain's offer'.[34] Board members noted, during one of the regular inspections of the depot, that in one room twenty girls were engaged in picking a fine sample of wheat.[35] A week later the wheat picking had been completed. 'The denizens of the depot are eager for further employment of this or any other kind whereby they might restore dilapidations in their apparel.'[36] It was reported in March that Tom Elder had employed some girls for grape picking at Myrtle Bank.[37] Also in March girls were employed in cleaning spoons that had been spotted with salt water.[38] Patrick Ennis told the Select Committee that current wages were 4/- or 5/- per week.[39] Girls in the depot were eager to earn some money and Matron Ross said that those who had been in the colony a long time 'are the most difficult to get rid of'.[40]

Health Care

Early in January 1856 it was reported to the FIB that two girls were ill with scurvy but were recovering, and there were no new cases.[41] They had been provided with cabbages and turnips and the Colonial Surgeon Dr James George Nash had changed the daily ration from rice to half a pound of potatoes.[42] Also, in early January Dr William Gosse was appointed Acting Colonial Surgeon and Superintendent of Lunatics during Nash's absence on leave. Since 1852 he had been an Honorary Medical Officer at the Adelaide Hospital. He reported to the Select Committee that he prescribed for between thirty and forty girls per day. The average was thirty, 'many trivial'.[43]

Dr Gosse was present for part of an FIB meeting early in February. He reported that more than ten per cent were sick in the depot and suggested a daily walk with Matron Ross and another nurse for the inmates of the sick ward.[44] An application was made by the nurse for Ward Six to have an additional nurse, as she was frequently disturbed in the night. Gosse acknowledged that another nurse was required and so the board approved and agreed that payment should be 5/- per week.[45]

A week later Gosse notified the board about the physical condition of the girls who had arrived on the *Lord Raglan*. He reported that there had been fever on board and several deaths during the voyage; and he 'feared danger from their admission into the depot, the inmates of which were in a state that would render them peculiarly liable to contract infection'.[46] However, despite a telegraphic message to the Port, the girls had already started their journey to Adelaide. Moorhouse remarked that it was impossible to keep such girls separated from the others.

At a meeting in March the FIB interviewed sixteen girls who had been in the colony for longer than twelve months. A few were too ill to be brought before the board. Most had been in service and had become ill, were readmitted, and were still under the care of a doctor. The board gave two weeks notice to all not certified as ill.[47]

In April ophthalmia was reported in the Central Depot where there were 138 residents.[48] There are no further reports of illness in the depot as the numbers of inmates decreased.

These examples indicate that the Colonial Government was diligent about providing what was considered at that time all necessary medical care in the Adelaide Depot.

The Closure of the Depot

There were reported to be 125 girls in the Adelaide Depot when the FIB held its last meeting at the end of April 1856. Numbers continued to decline from 107 in mid May to fifty-six in mid June.[49] There was a request for thirty pairs of boots from Moorhouse, who was acting in a voluntary capacity, in July. All girls were 'delicate, many having been in the sick ward for months and really have no means of purchasing boots' which had been recommended by the Colonial Surgeon.[50]

The *Government Gazette* of 8 August reported that there were twenty-nine female immigrants in the depot. On 4 September 1856 Moorhouse, former Superintendent, reported that eighteen females were now occupying the new female wards at the depot.

> A partition wall might be thrown across the yard and in one week the building might be ready to accommodate the military. Two or three rooms only would be set apart for the occupation of the single females.[51]

Excessive female immigration was no longer a problem in the colony.

CHAPTER THIRTEEN

From City to Country

Matthew Moorhouse reported that by the end of 1855 sixty-nine girls had been at the Adelaide Depot for over six months.[1] Many girls were fearful and unwilling to travel to isolated country areas. Efforts to find them employment in rural districts were consequently complicated and often drawn out.

In his September 1855 quarterly report the Immigration Agent Dr Handasyde Duncan wrote that a lot of single women seemed to have been selected for immigration who were not suited for domestic service. Anyone visiting rural districts of Ireland and Scotland knew females were employed in outdoor farm work. It is 'no degradation to make hay, or reap corn, milk cows or to manage details of the farmyard. It is that sort of work that a great many, now unemployed, are accustomed to.'[2] The clear implication was that many girls in the depot were not employable as domestic servants but only as farm servants.

Nevertheless there was difficulty inducing female immigrants in the Adelaide Depot to voluntarily leave town for country depots, as the Adelaide Depot was seen as a 'permanent home'. There is a memo from Moorhouse to Duncan dated 19 November 1855 in which he requests the Immigration Agent attend a special meeting of the board the next day to decide 'whether the girls who refused, before the board, to go to Clare, should be expelled'.[3] Moorhouse then wrote to the Colonial Secretary outlining the difficulties in some detail. He said that in mid November fifty girls had been needed for country depots – thirty for Clare, twelve for Mount Barker and eight for Gawler. However, only twelve could be induced to go by the Yard Supervisor. When he had reported this to the board, O'Halloran, who was acting as Chairman at this meeting, interviewed thirty-eight and met with thirty-four refusals. Moorhouse suggested, in his report to the Colonial Secretary, that the girls in the depot had been influenced by a letter received by one of them from a friend placed in the country who had indicated that wages were only 2/6 for heavy outdoor work. As Kingston was absent, the issue was deferred till the next meeting. At this meeting, on 20 November, Moorhouse wrote, girls entered the boardroom en masse and expressed regret for their earlier behaviour. (Imagine the discussions that were held in the intervening days in the depot, between matrons and girls, amongst the girls themselves and between those who had been longest in the depot and those who had been readmitted.) In recognition of this apology, Moorhouse reported, he then personally asked every girl, even those totally unsuited, to go to the country. After the meeting Michael Ryan had also visited every ward in an attempt to procure the necessary numbers.

Moorhouse illustrated further the 'insuperable difficulties' of getting girls into country depots by describing what happened repeatedly when a girl was selected for interview by a prospective employer. As soon as she heard about the low wages offered she would find such difficulties and appear to be so unsuited that the offer would be withdrawn.

The board's inability to enforce orders was further demonstrated by another example. Twelve girls were to go to the Mount Barker Depot by dray and everything was ready by 7 am. However the dray left at 2 pm with only ten aboard. Two had absconded![4]

The Governor's reply to Moorhouse's detailed report was to

advise the board that he would support them in any attempt to convince the immigrants that the depot was not their permanent home.[5] He had no suggestions and made no recommendations but later fully supported the closing of the gates and the establishment of a sentry box.

Moorhouse's memo was published in the press in response to questions asked by John Baker in the Legislative Council.[6] There was great public concern about the number of girls maintained, and about their behaviour. Comments were made also about the involvement of Catholic priests. The Colonial Secretary was forced to explain to the council members that priests tried to convince the girls to accept country positions.

There was certainly much disquiet amongst the girls themselves about going to the country. Mrs Patrick Ennis, Assistant Matron, mother of a child born the previous year and pregnant with her next, described country work to the Select Committee 'as drawing water from wells and attending to cattle and horses'.[7] Clearly, in her view, these were not the most preferred occupations. There was also difficulty in meeting the needs from country depots because there were incorrect reports regarding the girls' capabilities. 'There is scarcely one in the depot that will admit she is able to milk.' In December the Female Immigration Board (FIB) had decided that girls should be classified on board ship, prior to arrival at the depot, but that no girl unable to milk should be classified as a farm servant.[8]

One example of the girls' refusal to take country placement became notorious. A 13 December letter from Samuel Morcom, expressing anger and affront, was published in both the *Register* and the *Adelaide Observer*. 'I write this to give the public some idea of the behaviour of the girls now occupying the depot.' He and Mr Hutton had gone to the depot seeking three girls 'to enter service' at Gumeracha. They spent some time and examined, they said, about 300 girls but could not get one to go to a country place. 'A number expressed by their actions that they were not intending going out at all.' One girl, to Morcom's 'utter astonishment', threw a stone at him with great violence. He informed both Mr Moorhouse and Father Ryan, who were both there at the time, of the insult offered parties who had visited the depot.[9] In response to this publication Ambrose Newbold, Surgeon Superintendent on the barque *Agincourt*, wrote a letter dated 14 December to the *Register* saying that there were on board 'servants both ready and willing to go to the country'.

As no minutes of meetings held at this time are available, it is not known how the board attempted to improve this very poor public image of the Female Immigration Depot (FID). Subsequent decisions made were certainly less tolerant of the girls' preferences.

One girl was treated quite harshly. At the FIB meeting on 13 February, a letter was read from Mr Pearce of O'Halloran Hill who had gone to the Central Depot seeking a servant for a month, to milk and wash. He selected a girl and agreed to pay her 5/- per week, but she declined. She told the board, when called in, that she could not milk and that Mr Pearce had first said his wife would help, but then later said she was not well and could not. Other girls also refused, apparently because when he had visited the depot he was accompanied by three unruly young children, one crying. Matron Ross reported that his wife's illness was the reason Mr Pearce was trying to hire a servant. O'Halloran then told the girl who was first selected that she was a 'good for nothing girl, one who brought disgrace to her country'. Reverend Ryan thought it was a 'very gross case' and the girl was dismissed. She was eighteen years old, and had been in the colony 'about one month'.[10]

The same Mr Hutton from Gumeracha who had accompanied Mr Morcom to the depot in December, wrote to the board in response to Moorhouse's query about why Mary Berrigan had left his service. He claimed she had left against his wishes, but Mary told the board she had left with his consent, because she wanted to be nearer a chapel and priests. Mr Hutton asked for a replacement, 'free of expense', either English, Scottish or Welsh, who could milk, wash and do housework. The board found that it could not sanction Mary leaving on such grounds but, nevertheless, gave her a few days in the depot to find another place.[11]

The difficulties of getting girls to agree to move to the country continued for some months. It can only be assumed that girls initially went voluntarily to the country depots because they were ignorant of the distance to be travelled and of the isolation of country settlements. Patrick Ennis, the Yard Supervisor, born in 1822 in Dublin, had been resident in Goolwa[12] before his wife, Ann, had become the first Matron at Willunga. Because of her experience she had been transferred to the Adelaide Depot after the disturbance there. Patrick had consequently had contact with a great number of girls placed in immigrant depots. He told the Select Committee that 'a great many girls had left their father's house to come here, without ever having been in service'.[13] At an FIB meeting in March, Ennis reported that girls had been making false claims. Girls describing themselves as farm servants, when questioned by potential employers said they could not milk – to avoid being employed in the country.[14] The board agreed that a new list be drawn up and that girls would be dismissed for making false claims.[15]

The number of single female immigrants arriving declined significantly in the summer months. The harvest for 1855–1856 was plentiful, much better than the previous year. On 31 December, two ships arrived, the *Nimrod* (121 domestic servants) and the *Fitzjames* (157), increasing the numbers in the depot. Another 140 were returned from temporary harvest work, so that on 28 January 414 girls were recorded as resident in the Adelaide Depot.[16] By early March the number had fallen to 277.[17]

The declining number of girls requiring employment and the closure of many of the country depots meant that country placements were far less frequent. In March Moorhouse said that all the girls in the Adelaide Depot at that time were re-admissions. Ward Eight was to be closed and used as a store.[18] At an FIB meeting in mid April, Patrick Ennis reported that the rule making removal to country depots a condition of entry was working well.[19] Apparently those girls who did not wish to be sent to the country could now find themselves positions in the city. By that time very few girls were being sent to Mount Barker or Encounter Bay, and Kapunda Depot was the only remaining active country resource.

CHAPTER FOURTEEN

Readmission: A Contentious Issue

When Matthew Moorhouse recommended the establishment of a Female Immigration Board (FIB), he wrote of the need for a policy regarding readmission, already a contentious issue. If the girls 'are made too comfortable they will not remain in situations, they will throw themselves on the merest pretext upon government and be quite contented to remain'. Moorhouse even discussed the quality of the food provided.

> Some would argue that vegetables and condiments should be allowed for soup – others would maintain that these luxuries are not always procurable at out-stations even by the affluent settlers and shouldn't be allowed in town.[1]

Once the board started meeting, members immediately asked the Governor for direction in devising a policy for the readmission of girls who had been in the colony over twelve months. The Governor responded adroitly by saying that such matters were for the board to determine. His opinion was that girls who had been given fair opportunity of earning a livelihood should not be readmitted – unless there was illness or some other misfortune.[2] 'The knowledge that such permission will be granted prevents them from making adequate exertions to better themselves.'[3] The Governor felt that to avoid the very real danger of the depots turning into 'a poorhouse', great exertions would be required. 'The growth of a permanent pauperism – the worst blight which can fall on a new country' would necessitate the establishment of very tough regulations about readmission.[4]

The issue of readmission to the various depots of girls who had left 'for service' was complex and caused much friction between the Governor and the board. This conflict emerged very quickly after the establishment of the board and was never resolved.

Minutes of the board meetings were not kept and so only a few decisions were made public until meetings were opened to the press at the end of the year. At the FIB meeting on 27 December, it was agreed that the meetings could be reported. (Meetings of the Destitute Board were not open to the press until February 1856.) A reporter from the *Adelaide Observer* who, at the next meeting, accompanied the FIB on its regular inspection of the Adelaide Depot, observed a large, central refectory for the girls. It was well away from their dormitories which were clean and comfortable, each accommodating fifty–sixty girls, and each with a Matron in charge. On the opposite side of the courtyard there was a long, narrow and far less comfortable room which was for readmitted girls.[5] Clearly every possible disincentive was used to deter readmission, no matter how justified.

Matron Ross told the Select Committee: 'There are so many persons who take girls for a week and if not suited then they are sent away.' She felt that a week was not long enough and the girls had not been given a fair trial. Mrs Ennis would recommend a minimum term of employment. Three months had been the usual period at Willunga.[6]

At a meeting in January, the Governor accompanied the board in its usual visitation of the wards, preceding its meeting. It was noted that there were twenty girls in the infirmary, none dangerously ill.[7] In the dormitory for readmitted girls he asked one why she had left her place. She said her master was Mr

Barnitt (Barritt?) of Ayer's Flat. One newspaper reported that she had to milk seven cows,[8] two others that it was eleven.[9] She had to wash for up to a dozen people, as well as doing housework and fieldwork. She had remained as long as she was able, but then 'broke down'. She showed her hands, which looked as if 'coated in horns';[10] cracked and cut all over with the skin nearly entirely peeled off.[11] Patrick Ennis reported to the Select Committee about a month later that she had 'since gone to a situation'.[12] Presumably her injured hands had recovered.

Applications for readmission, which were considered at every hearing, were described with relish in both daily papers and the weekly *Adelaide Observer*. The issue became very public and once again the Governor's authority was defied. Early in January the FIB approved a circular for country depots about readmission after harvest, prepared by Moorhouse.

> There will be many applicants for readmission after harvest, but the government are anxious to prevent as much as possible any readmission, therefore readmit only those specially taken for harvest or other work with distinct understanding that they would be returned on completion of such service.[13]

O'Halloran had suggested that no more girls be sent to country depots, because it was anticipated that most would be returned. Moorhouse agreed that no more should be sent to Clare but felt that plenty more would be needed at Mount Barker and Kapunda.[14] In a memorandum on 9 January 1856, Governor MacDonnell objected strongly to the FIB circular. He did not want to give power to Matrons to readmit girls hired specially for short periods. This was, he wrote, 'opposed to what ought to be the primary object of the board, viz., the permanent settlement and dispersing of the immigrants amongst the general mass of the population.' A great effort should be made, in the heart of the harvest, to 'get rid of' the immigrants. He felt that farmers and other employers would be encouraged to use the service of these girls for only short periods and then return them to be maintained at the expense of the public for many months until required again. Similarly, girls would not be encouraged to find permanent employment if they knew they could return to a 'comfortable home and good diet'. The majority of the Irish female immigrants were accustomed to outdoor farm work, and 'enlisting the utmost exertions of the girls themselves' could not be achieved unless 'they are made to feel and understand that once they leave the depot, its door is shut to them for ever'. Governor MacDonnell suggested that if a Matron readmitted anyone, under special circumstances, the cost of the girl's rations should be deducted from her salary.[15]

The board's reply, dated 21 January, was lengthy and abrasive. The number of unprotected females was far in excess of present demand for servants, and for the sake of morality and ordinary humanity it was the duty of government to find shelter and sustenance for them. No general rule could be framed for a policy of readmission. Every case had to be decided 'on its own merits'. Should the present stream of immigrants be arrested the 'serious evil will remedy itself ere the lapse of many months'. The constant fluctuations of the labour market, and the prosperous state of the agriculture community 'for whose service a majority of the girls is more especially suited' justified the board's readmission policy. Figures were provided that indicated that over a period of a little more than three months, 1343 females had been sent from the depot. The board considered a policy of refusal to readmit to be 'highly impolitic, unjust and cruel'. Arguments were presented which were extremely emotional. Many girls without money, home or friends would be forced into prostitution, or become inmates of the Destitute Asylum, from which they were unlikely to be employed. Moorhouse neatly reversed his choice of adjectives, to state that the practice of readmitting the 'deserving' to the Central Depot is 'politic, just and merciful'. The board 'urgently advocate its continuance under the present system'.[16] The 'unworthy' were, of course, excluded.

When discussing the Governor's response to the circular, before the board's reply was written, Kingston remarked that the public was not aware that farmers were replacing hard-working men with girls. Girls could be hired for 3/- or 4/- per week – amounts that would have to be paid daily to men. The work required was sometimes enormous as many examples that had come before them would testify. Kingston was not proposing the concept of equal pay for equal work but clearly he was concerned about exploitation.[17] O'Halloran felt that the board could not be stricter without forcing girls to make a choice between overwork and prostitution.

During the several weeks that the FIB took to draft its reply to the Governor's memorandum, only a few cases were refused readmission, until further information became available. At the meeting on 12 January Honora Ryan was readmitted. She had accepted two places; the last for nine weeks with a Mrs Murphy of North Adelaide who had constantly abused and ill-treated her, dismissing her without notice. At the next meeting Honora was brought before the board with Mrs Murphy, who did not deny that she had called the girl names – after provocation. She said Honora had left without notice after only a warning. The board decided that the girl had been insolent and badly behaved, and she was dismissed from the depot. One paper reported that she had already been readmitted three times.[18] Another claimed that Reverend Ryan had disagreed with the decision, saying that the girl herself had been provoked.[19]

Rose Dunn, who had been hired from the Willunga Depot – which was by now closed – and dismissed on the same day because she could not reap, had found work at the Horseshoe Inn on her way back to the depot. However, she was no longer required at the inn, had good character, and so was readmitted.[20] She had been paid 5/- per week and had to pay 8/- for her fare into town.[21] At an FIB meeting early in February, Joseph Boothy from the Horseshoe Inn complained because Rose Dunn had been readmitted after she had told the board she was no longer wanted, at a meeting several weeks before. He said she had taken leave of absence because she was sick, and had promised to return. He had kept her position open and had only hired another girl after he had read in the paper that Rose had been readmitted. Rose was brought before the board, 'prevaricated very grossly', could not deny the facts and so was dismissed.[22] In both these examples readmission was temporary until evidence could be provided to enable decisions to be finalised.

Ellen Decourcy was readmitted, with a warning, after she had left a situation. She said she was 'quite competent' but had not been furnished with the proper appliances for washing.[23] Most of her fellow applicants were not as fortunate. One was Mary Bolton who applied for readmission on 19 November 1855. She had been required to drive horses to water and to fill the trough with a pump. The board felt she was quite able to do such work, and because she had not given her employer more than four days' trial, they dismissed her.[24] Another was Margaret Walsh who had been in a situation with Mr R. Hawkes, and said she had left because of ill health. Because she had no character reference she was refused readmission.[25] One girl was dismissed for refusing a situation at 5/- per week, providing for only two people.[26] There were similar cases but little detail provided in any of the newspapers. Without board meeting minutes it is impossible to determine the accuracy of these journalistic reports. There is clear evidence that discharge letters or character references were pivotal for assessments.

On 24 January the *Adelaide Times* reported that at the meeting on the previous day there were many other cases of readmission 'of no possible interest.' By the date of the following meeting an additional 161 girls had been admitted to the depot from aboard ship, so there was additional pressure on the board to limit readmissions. Nevertheless, decisions seem to have been fair and consistent, albeit sometimes harsh. Ann Lowry was refused admission because she could not produce a discharge.[27] She claimed that her late master preferred English girls – a claim the board said she had made frequently. Catherine Cassidy, who applied because of ill health, also had no discharge letter but said that no one in her employer's family could write. She was admitted pending a medical certificate.[28] Another girl, M. Hallion, was readmitted because she had been returned 'unsuited to German habits'.[29]

Figures provided in January 1856 showing the number of female immigrants admitted and 'disposed of' since the second meeting of the board (8 October), revealed that 1595 girls had been admitted to the Adelaide Depot and that 1343 had left for service, including 275 from country depots. Only 252 remained; 509 had been readmitted.[30]

Two girls with excellent characters were refused readmission because they had been over twelve months in the colony. It was reported that the girls, Eliza Keogh and C. Casheen, left the board meeting crying bitterly.[31] The *Register* reported that a neat, modest-looking girl asked what she should do.[32] At the next meeting O'Halloran objected to turning away those girls who had been in the colony longer than twelve months. He found it painful, and referred to three who had been turned away crying. The board agreed to direct the clerk not to let such girls apply.[33] Brigid Keogh, from Galway, who had arrived in January 1855 on the *Coromandel*, told the Committee of Enquiry that she had operated a school with her sister before emigrating. She had been in service for eight months at Brompton until she was no longer wanted. She had then lived at Thebarton with a shipmate, looking for a situation, until lack of money forced her to return to the Adelaide Depot. She had not been in a country depot. She may very well have been Eliza's sister.[34]

Early in February sixty-two females were admitted from onboard ship,[35] so again numbers were temporarily augmented in the Adelaide Depot. However, only a month later Moorhouse reported that all girls in the depot were readmissions.[36] Clearly job opportunities were improving.

Jane Callilay was readmitted from the London Coffee House, Hindley Street, called a 'board and lodging house, which she described as a house of disrepute'. She had noticed that one girl, who had been a shipmate and had been turned out of the depot for improper conduct, had stopped all night in the company of a gentleman.[37] It was this Jane who was then sent to the Mount Barker Depot, was dismissed for calling Matron Frankpitt a liar, and was brought before the board again in March, applying for another readmission.[38] Fortunately she was hired out before the board reached a determination.

It was not until the end of February that girls could be readmitted to the depot temporarily, pending a hearing by the board. Members were uncomfortable about those girls who were left stranded, homeless and without resources. At one board meeting O'Halloran referred to a letter, published in the *Adelaide Times* about a girl who had been employed for one week and was then dismissed, having earned 3/-. The letter described the difficulties she experienced because she could not be considered for readmission until the board next sat. O'Halloran said he had understood that Moorhouse had admitted girls provisionally. (No reference was made to the occasion when the Reverend Ryan had permitted Mary Reagan from the Encounter Bay Depot temporary accommodation prior to an FIB meeting very early in the year!) Moorhouse was adamant that he had never admitted any able-bodied applicant for readmission, under any circumstance.

Dr Duncan gave another example of the need for more flexibility. A woman who lived on the Port Road engaged one young girl from the depot. When the employer arrived home with the girl her husband refused to allow her to hire a servant and so lodging had to be obtained for the girl. Duncan trusted that the depot would accommodate her even though she had no discharge letter.[39] After a long discussion it was eventually agreed that Moorhouse and Ryan, together, should use their discretion to temporarily readmit prior to meeting days.[40]

At the same meeting (23 February 1856) the board, in response to requests from those wishing to avoid publicity, decided that names of both employer and servants would be withheld.

Readmission became far more difficult as the board established more and more stringent requirements. At the board meeting of 23 February it was reported that thirty-six had applied for readmission and thirty-five of these had written discharge recommendations.[41] At a meeting two weeks later it was reported that 'a great many girls besieged the doors of the Boardroom seeking admission'. The board reiterated its policy of saying no to all girls who left situations without good cause, to those who were discharged for misconduct, those who had been more than twelve months in the colony, and any who had been repeatedly discharged.[42]

For some women, being scrutinised whilst appearing before the board was very frightening. A governess, who had been temporarily readmitted, refused to go before the board and was summarily dismissed.[43]

In March the board investigated the cases of those girls already in the depot – the number varies from one newspaper report to another – who had been in the colony for over twelve months, and a fortnight later recalled the twelve who remained. Seven had been hired and of the remaining five, those without doctor's certificates were dismissed.[44]

There were several examples of the board providing protection. Approval was given for a girl to refuse a situation with a man, two children and no wife.[45] Another was readmitted after being placed in a house of bad character, 'one of Mr Peacock's cottages behind the Post Office.'[46] One fifteen-year-old was considered too young to wash and work for a family of eleven and she was readmitted.[47] Another 'very young girl' was readmitted from the country where she had been required to milk four cows, wash for eight people and do housework – all for 2/6 per week. The work was considered 'too much' for her.[48]

By early April, four depots – Willunga, Clare, Robe and Gawler – had been closed, and Kapunda had been opened. Only three other country facilities remained and two of these were in the process of closing. The board therefore had fewer resources than when it was established in October. At the time, when the number of unemployed female arrivals declined so too did the number of applicants for readmission. Nevertheless the board determined that placement in a country depot become a condition of readmission. This stringent policy may very well have been a major contributing factor to deter girls from 'besieging the gates', seeking readmission as they had done early in March. However, economic conditions also improved in the colony and servant girls were better able to find themselves positions in the city. By the end of April, when the board last sat, the policing of readmissions was no longer a contentious issue. There was not, any more, an excess of female Irish immigrants.

CHAPTER FIFTEEN

Conclusion

Immigration depots were not unique to South Australia. One had been operating from the barracks at Hyde Park in Sydney since the late 1840s. The establishment of servants depots in South Australian country areas, however, reveals that this Colonial Government took responsibility for caring for the influx of unemployable female immigrants with a great deal of pragmatism and some imagination. The provision of an acceptable standard of accommodation, food and medical care in the Central Depot and the development of adequate resources for country depots indicates that the government was serious about its duty of care.

The establishment of a board to legitimise decisions about where women were to be sent reflects an enlightened, 'liberal' administration of a colony with no convicts. Members of the Female Immigration Board (FIB) showed themselves to be diligent and well intentioned. They made intelligent appraisals of the seasonal demands for labour. They argued that temporary employment at harvest time necessitated readmission of discharged girls to the depots for their own safety, and advised country depots of this policy in a carefully worded circular. On this issue the board members were quite prepared to challenge Governor MacDonnell's directives in order to protect girls for whom they were responsible. In addition, members were well aware that females were much cheaper to employ than male farm labourers and tried not to place girls in positions where they would have to choose between accepting exploitative, harsh working conditions and being expelled from a depot, rendering them unemployed and homeless. It has been shown that members tried to protect girls from dismissal because they saw prostitution as an almost inevitable consequence. The board's attempts to induce girls, despite their objections, to go to country depots where the potential for employment was much greater than in Adelaide, well illustrates the underlying paternalism which permeated decisions. Today, enticing young people to country locations is still difficult.

The operation of the depots illustrates, obliquely, early attempts at industrial action in the colony. It has been shown that the Matron of the Clare Depot was quickly prevented from advising girls to refuse to take work for minimal wages and was threatened with dismissal. The fracas at the Willunga Depot was the consequence of the attempts by the local priest and the Matron to protect girls from poor wages and religious intolerance. At every depot efforts were made to ensure a degree of job security for those who had been hired. For example, at the Encounter Bay Depot landowners were expected to employ girls for at least six months, a policy which provoked some heated objections by potential employers. At Robe the Matron was pleased to report that some girls were hired for twelve months, and none for less than three months. Similarly unfair dismissal was not tolerated. The Matron at Mount Barker several times recovered wages for girls who had not been paid and ensured that girls were re-employed after being discharged inappropriately. Conditions of employment were also considered. Again, it was the Mount Barker Matron who refused to send a girl to a house of reputed drunkards.

Although limited, the information available about those who arrived in 1855 and were placed in servants depots indicates that they were, in general, fairly treated. Ellen Moore was well looked after, despite being shipwrecked and subsequently accommodated in two temporary facilities before enduring an uncomfortable, wet trip by bullock dray to a newly established, poorly furnished depot at Clare. She was employed very quickly. Her experience exemplifies the efforts which were continually made to provide for the excess of female immigrants.

NOTES

Guide to endnote abbreviations

ADB	*Australian Dictionary of Biography*, vol. 2, 1851–1890
AJCP	Australian Joint Copying Project
AO	*Adelaide Observer*
AT	*Adelaide Times*
BI	*Biographical Index of South Australia, 1836–1885*
CO	Colonial Office
CSO	Colonial Secretary's Office
GRG	General Records Group
GRG 28	Destitute Persons Department
GRG 35/301	*Irish Female Immigration, Details of Expenditure at Adelaide and at the various country depots*
GRG 35/43	Immigration Agent's Correspondence
GRG 4/58	Local Courts, Mount Barker
JACHS	*Journal of the Australian Catholic Historical Society*
JHSSA	Historical Society of South Australia, journal
MRG	Municipal Records Group
Reg	*South Australian Register*
SAGG	*South Australian Government Gazette*
SALC	South Australia Legislative Council
SAPP	South Australia Parliamentary Papers
SCR	South Australia Legislative Council, *Report of the Select Committee appointed to enquire into Excessive Female Immigration; together* SCR M *with Minutes of evidence and Appendix*
SRSA	State Records of South Australia
SRSA RN	State Records of South Australia, Research Notes

Notes to Chapter 1

1 AJCP CO 13/90/35
2 SAGG, 12 July 1855, p. 515
3 ADB 1851–1890, p. 148
4 Harcus, W., ed., *South Australia: Its History, Resources and Productions*, Cox, Adelaide, 1876, p. 8.
5 Loyau, G., *The Representative Men of South Australia*, G. Howell, Adelaide, 1883, p. 18.
6 AJCP CO 13/90
7 GRG 35/46/16
8 AJCP CO 13/91/46
9 GRG CSO 24/6/1855/2441
10 AJCP CO 13/91/46
11 ALCP CO 13/91/46
12 AO 14/7/1855
13 AJCP CO 13/90/237
14 SAGG, 12 July 1855, p. 515
15 AJCP CO 13/90/280
16 AJCP CO 13/90, pp. 248–250
17 SCR M, p. 37
18 SAGG 18/12/56
19 AJCP CO 13/91/27
20 AJCP CO 13/91/132
21 AJCP CO 13/92/99
22 AJCP CO 13/93
23 SCR App, p. ii
24 Reg 3/3/1856
25 Reg 25/2/1856
26 GRG CSO 24/90/179
27 SCR App, p. ii
28 Haines, R., 'Government Assisted Immigration from the United Kingdom to Australia 1831–1860: Promotion, Recruitment and the Labouring Poor', PhD Thesis, Flinders University, 1992, p. 534.

Notes to Chapter 2

1 Reg 8/3/1855
2 Parkin, C.W., 'Irish Female Immigration to South Australia during the Great Famine', BA Thesis, University of Adelaide, 1964, p. 85.
3 AT 12/7/1855.
4 GRG CSO 24/6/1855/332.
5 GRG CSO 24/6/1855/3452.
6 GRG CSO 24/6/1855/2751.
7 GRG CSO 24/6/1855/658.
8 GRG CSO 24/20/1855/97.
9 GRG CSO 28/1/6/105.
10 Dickey, B., *Rations, Residence, Resources*, Wakefield Press, Adelaide, 1986, p. 28.
11 GRG CSO 24/6/1855/3112.
12 GRG CSO 24/6/1855/3112.
13 GRG CSO 24/6/1855/3111.
14 GRG CSO 24/6/1855/2986.
15 GRG CSO 24/20/1855/170.
16 GRG CSO 24/20/1855/184.
17 GRG CSO 24/6/1855/4035.
18 GRG CSO 24/6/1855/3452.

Notes to Chapter 3

1 GRG CSO 24/4/1855/706.
2 AO, Supp, 15/9/1855.
3 AT 13/9/1855.
4 CSO GRG 24/6/1855/2996.

Notes to Chapter 4

1 AJCP CO 13/91/48.
2 SAGG 1854, p. 322.
3 GRG CSO 24/6/1855/3112.
4 Pike, ADB, 1851–1890.
5 Reg 31/1/1856.

6 Pike, ADB, 1851–1890.
7 Steiner, Marie, 'Michael Ryan and the Female Immigration Board in South Australia', *Journal of the Australian Catholic Historical Society*, vol. 24, 2003, p. 57.
8 SAGG 20/6/1839.
9 GRG CSO 24/4/1855/66.
10 Steiner, Marie, 'Matthew Moorhouse: A Controversial Colonist', Historical Society of South Australia, no. 31, 2003, p. 55.
11 GRG CSO 24/6/1855/3369.
12 GRG CSO 24/6/1855/3695.
13 GRG CSO 24/6/1856/146.
14 SAGG 31/1/1856.
15 GRG CSO 24/6/1856/1460.
16 GRG CSO 24/6/1856/1179.
17 GRG CSO 24/6/1856/1459.
18 SCR Appx1.

Notes to Chapter 5

1 Willunga Progress Association, *Willunga: 'Place of Green Trees'*, Adelaide, nd, p. 38.
2 GRG CSO 24/4/1855/472.
3 GRG CSO 24/6/1855/2063.
4 GRG CSO 24/6/1855/3206.
5 Reg 9/1/1856.
6 GRG CSO 24/4/1855/472.
7 GRG CSO 24/6/1855/2270.
8 GRG CSO 24/6/1855/2408.
9 SCR M, p. 28.
10 SALC, Willunga Immigrant Depot, Correspondence, 24/2/1856.
11 AJCP CO 13/91/47.
12 GRG CSO 24/6/1855/3468.
13 GRG CSO 24/6/1855/3696.
14 GRG CSO 24/5/44/3731.
15 GRG 5/2/685.
16 GRG 35/301.

Notes to Chapter 6

1 Noye, R.J., *Clare: A District History*, Lynton Publications, Coromandel Valley, 1975, p. 14.
2 GRG CSO 24/6/1855/3345.
3 GRG CSO 24/20/1855/191.
4 SCR M, p. 11.
5 GRG CSO 24/6/1855/2431.
6 GRG CSO 24/6/1855/3043.
7 GRG CSO 24/6/1855/2431.
8 Ibid.
9 AO 11/8/1855.
10 GRG CSO 24/6/1855/2748.
11 GRG CSO 24/6/1855/2431.
12 GRG CSO 24/6/1855/3345.
13 AJCP CO 13/91.
14 Reg 3/1/1856.
15 Reg 11/2/1856.
16 AT 11/2/1856.
17 Reg 11/2/1856.
18 AT 1611856.
19 AT 22/1/1856.
20 GRG CSO 24/6/1855/2431.
21 AT 28/1/1856.
22 GRG, Register of Cases of Destitution, 28/4.
23 Catholic Archives, Sevenhills Register of Marriages, 1849–1858.
24 SA Births Index of Register 1842–1906.
25 Ibid.
26 Reg 11/2/1856.
27 GRG 35/301.
28 GRG 28/4.
29 GRG 35/301.

30 Reg 4/2/1856.
31 GRG 35/301.
32 Reg 14/2/1856.
33 Reg 25/2/1856.
34 Reg 3/3/1856.
35 Reg 17/3/1856.
36 Reg 31/3/1856.

Notes to Chapter 7

1 Bermingham, K., *Gateway to the South East*, South East Times, Millicent, 1961, p. 202.
2 Ibid., p. 172.
3 McClean, C., 'Dr Handasyde Duncan as Immigration Agent in SA: 1853–1878', BA Thesis, Flinders University, 1992, p. 15.
4 GRG CSO 24/6/1855/2205.
5 GRG CSO 24/6/1855/2531.
6 Bermingham, K., *Gateway to the South East*, p. 123.
7 Ibid., p. 125.
8 GRG CSO 24/6/1855/2812.
9 Ibid.
10 GRG CSO 24/4/1855/892.
11 GRG CSO 24/4/1856/283.
12 AT 17/1/1856.
13 GRG CSO 24/6/1855/4046.
14 GRG CSO 24/6/1856/1460.
15 GRG CSO 24/6/1855/2969.
16 GRG CSO 24/6/1855/3109.
17 GRG CSO 24/6/1855/3904.
18 GRG CSO 24/6/1856/11.
19 GRG CSO 24/6/1856/140.
20 GRG CSO 24/6/1855/4180.
21 Reg 14/2/1856.
22 Reg 4/2/1856.
23 Reg 25/2/1856.
24 26 according to SRSA Research Notes, vol. 5, p. 236.
25 Bermingham, K., *Gateway to the South East*, p. 171.
26 Reg 31/3/1856.
27 GRG CSO 24/6/1856/906.
28 Bermingham, K., *Gateway to the South East*, p. 125.
29 AO 26/1/1856.

Notes to Chapter 8

1 Whitelock, D., *Gawler*, Corporation of the Town of Gawler, 1989, p. 212.
2 SAGG 2/7/1856.
3 SAGG 16/3/1856.
4 Loyau, G., *The Gawler Handbook including the memoirs of Dr Nott*, Adelaide, Goodfellow & Hele, 1880, p. 10.
5 MRG 43/1/1 3, 9, 30 July 1855.
6 GRG CSO 24/6/2855/2597.
7 GRG CSO 24/6/1855/3508.
8 GRG 35/301.
9 Whitelock, D., *Gawler*, p. 49.
10 Ibid., p. 24.
11 BI.
12 GRG CSO 24/6/1855/2790½.
13 GRG CSO 24/6/1855/2854.
14 AT 25/8/1855.
15 GRG CSO 24/6/1855/2854.
16 GRG CSO 24/6/1855/3239.
17 AO 5/1/1856.
18 AO 2/2/1856.
19 AT 28/1/1856.
20 GRG 28/4.
21 Reg 21/12/1855.
22 Reg 26/12/1855.
23 GRG CSO 24/6/1855/3732.
24 AO 5/1/1856.
25 SCR M, p. 11.

26 AT 14/1/1856
27 AO 26/1/1856
28 GRG 28/14
29 Reg 21/1/1856
30 Reg 4/2/1856
31 GRG CSO 24/6/1855/3508
32 Reg 14/2/1856
33 Reg 31/12/1855
34 Reg 4/2/1856
35 Reg 25/2/1856
36 Coombe, E.H., *History of Gawler 1837–1908*, facsimile, Gawler Institute, 1978, p. 24.

Notes to Chapter 9

1 Laube, A., *Settlers Around the Bay: The Pioneering Families of Encounter Bay and Victor Harbor*, Laube, Adelaide, 1985, p. 3.
2 SAGG 14/2/1856.
3 Reg 9/1/2856.
4 GRG 35/301.
5 Hodge, Charles R., *Encounter Bay: The Miniature Naples of South Australia*, C. Hodge, Adelaide, 1932, p. 84.
6 GRG CSO 24/20/1855/137.
7 GRG 35/43.
8 GRG CSO 24/6/1855/3458.
9 Reg 3/11/1855.
10 Reg 16/11/1855.
11 Reg 1/12/1855.
12 Reg 13/1/1856.
13 AT 31/1/1856.
14 AO 2/2/1856.
15 GRG 35/301.
16 AO 14/1/1856.
17 AT 17/1/1856.
18 AT 24/1/1856.
19 Reg 21/1/1856.
20 AO 26/1/1856.
21 Reg 28/1/1856.
22 AT 24/1/1856.
23 Reg 4/2/1856.
24 AT 11/2/1856.
25 AT 25/2/1856.
26 Reg 25/2/1856.
27 Reg 10/3/1856.
28 AT 10/3/1856.
29 Reg 31/3/1856.
30 Reg 14/4/1856.
31 GRG CSO 24/6/1855/156.
32 GRG CSO 24/6/1856/1617.

Notes to Chapter 10

1 SAGCR 12/1/1839.
2 Martin, V., *Mostly Mount Barker*, Martin, Adelaide, 1982, p 19.
3 Herriman, A., 'Irish Settlers beyond the Tiers, Mount Barker, South Australia 1836-1886', unpublished abstract.
4 Dunn, J., p. 53.
5 Schmidt, B., p. 75.
6 MRG 43/1/1 9/7/1855.
7 Herriman, A., 'Irish Girls Defend Their Honour and Their Rights', paper presented to the Historical Society of South Australia, 2 July 1999.
8 GRG 35/301.
9 Herriman, A., 'Irish Girls'.
10 Ibid.
11 SCR M, p. 20.
12 Schmidt, B., *Mountain Upon the Plain: A History of Mount Barker and Its Surroundings*, District Council of Mount Barker, 1983, p. 81.
13 SAGG 13/3/1856.
14 SAGG 1856 p 457.

15 Reg 8/11/1855.
16 MRG 43/1/1 10/12/1855.
17 GRG 35/301.
18 AO 5/1/1856.
19 AT 7/1/1856.
20 AT 31/1/1856.
21 AO 2/2/1856.
22 Reg 18/2/1856.
23 GRG 35/301.
24 AT 18/2/1856.
25 GRG 35/301.
26 Ibid.
27 Reg 3/1/1856.
28 Reg 10/1/1856.
29 AT 14/1/1856.
30 AO 19/1/1856.
31 SCR M, p. 30.
32 AO 19/1/1856.
33 AT 22/1/1856.
34 Reg 21/1/1856.
35 Reg 28/1/1856.
36 Reg 25/2/1856.
37 SCR M, p. 20.
38 Reg 3/3/1856.
39 AT 10/3/1856.
40 Reg 10/3/1856.
41 AT 10/3/1856.
42 AT 7/4/1856.
43 Reg 31/3/1856.
44 Ibid.
45 AT 24/1/1856.
46 GRG 4/58/2.
47 Herriman, A., 'Irish Girls'.
48 Ibid.

Notes to Chapter 11

1 Kapunda District Council, *Kapunda. Centenary Celebrations, 1946.*
2 Charlton, R., *The History of Kapunda*, Hawthorn Press, Melbourne, 1971, p. 18.
3 Ibid., p. 74.
4 GRG CSO 24/6/1856/2422.
5 AT 31/1/1856.
6 Charlton, R., p. 66.
7 AT 6/2/1856.
8 GRG 35/301.
9 Reg 6/2/1856.
10 Reg 18/2/1856.
11 AT 4/2/1856.
12 Reg 14/2/1856.
13 Reg 25/2/1856.
14 GRG 35/301.
15 Reg 3/3/1856.
16 AT 3/3/1856.
17 GRG 35/301.
18 Reg 14/2/1856.
19 Reg 31/3/1856.
20 Reg 21/4/1856.
21 Reg 14/4/1856.
22 GRG CSO 24/6/1856/1455.
23 GRG CSO 24/5/1856/2422.
24 GRG 35/301.

Notes to Chapter 12

1 SCR M, p. 22.
2 GRG CSO 24/20/1855/97.
3 Parkin, C., 'Irish Female Immigration to South Australia during the Great Famine', BA Thesis, University of Adelaide, 1964, p. 95.
4 AO 19/1/1856.
5 GRG CSO 24/6/1856/141.
6 AT 7/1/1856.
7 AO 19/1/1856.
8 Reg 28/2/1856.
9 Reg 3/3/1856.

10 GRG CSO 24/6/1856/2643.
11 Reg 17/12/1855.
12 Reg 21/12/1855.
13 GRG CSO 24/6/1855/3955.
14 GRG CSO 24/6/1855/4166.
15 GRG CSO 24/20/1855/261.
16 GRG CSO 24/6/1855/4166.
17 Reg 28/12/1855.
18 Reg 21/12/1855.
19 Reg 3/1/1856.
20 AT 28/1/1856.
21 Reg 4/2/1856.
22 SCR M, p. 37.
23 Reg 4/2/1856.
24 SCR, App xi.
25 SCR M, p. 21.
26 AO 5/1/1856
27 Reg 21/12/1855.
28 AT 10/1/1856.
29 Reg 10/1/1856.
30 AO 26/1/1856.
31 AT 10/3/1856.
32 SCR M, p. 26.
33 Reg 4/2/1856.
34 GRG CSO 24/4/1856/59.
35 Reg 25/2/1856.
36 Reg 3/3/1856.
37 Reg 31/3/1856.
38 Reg 17/3/1856.
39 SCR M, p. 27.
40 SCR M, p. 20.
41 AT 7/1/1856.
42 Reg 3/1/1856.
43 SCR M, p. 29.
44 Reg 4/2/1856.
45 GRG CSO 24/6/1856/49.
46 Reg 14/2/1856.
47 Reg 3/3/1856.
48 Reg 14/4/1856.
49 SAGG 1856, p. 561.
50 GRG CSO 24/6/1856/2355.
51 GRG CSO 24/6/1856/2850.

Notes to Chapter 13

1 SAPP 1855–1856, no. 86.
2 Reg 20/10/1855.
3 GRG 35/43.
4 Reg 21/12/1855.
5 GRG CSO 24/4/1855/900.
6 Reg 21/12/1855.
7 SCR M, p. 27.
8 GRG 35/42.
9 Reg 14/12/1855.
10 Reg 15/2/1856.
11 Reg 25/2/1856.
12 BI.
13 SCR M, p. 26.
14 Reg 10/3/1856.
15 AT 10/3/1856.
16 Reg 29/1/1856.
17 SAGG 6/3/1856.
18 AT 10/3/1856.
19 Reg 14/4/1856.

Notes to Chapter 14

1 GRG CSO 24/6/1855/3112.
2 GRG CSO 24/6/1855/3333.
3 GRG CSO 24/4/1855/779.
4 GRG CSO 24/6/1855/3369.
5 AO 5/1/1856.
6 SCR M, p. 28.
7 AO 19/1/1856.
8 AT 14/1/1856.
9 Reg 14/1/1856.
10 AO 19/1/1856.
11 AT 14/1/1856.
12 SCR M, p. 26.
13 AT 7/1/1856.
14 Reg 3/1/1856.

15 SALC, Female Immigrant Depot, paper 95, 23/1/56.
16 GRG CSO 24/6/1855/228.
17 AT 14/1/1856.
18 AO 19/1/1856.
19 AT 17/1/1856.
20 AT 14/1/1856.
21 Reg 14/1/1856.
22 Reg 4/2/1856.
23 Reg 14/1/1856.
24 AT 22/1/1856.
25 AO 26/1/1856.
26 AT 4/2/1856.
27 Reg 28/1/1856
28 Ibid.
29 AT 28/1/1856.
30 GRG CSO 24/6/1855/228.
31 AT 6/2/1856.
32 Reg 6/2/1856.
33 Reg 11/2/1856.
34 SCR M, p. 38.
35 AT 11/2/1856.
36 AT 10/3/1856.
37 AT 11/2/1856.
38 AT 7/4/1856.
39 Reg 25/2/1856.
40 AT 25/2/1856.
41 Reg 25/2/1856.
42 Reg 10/3/1856.
43 AT 25/2/1856.
44 AT 16/3/1856.
45 Reg 3/3/1856.
46 Reg 14/2/1856.
47 AT 31/3/1856.
48 Reg 11/2/1856.

APPENDIX ONE

Servant Girl Passengers on the *Nashwauk*

This information is based on Janet Callen's book, *What Really Happened to the* Nashwauk? It is derived from specific documents – the *Nominal List of Emigrants on board the Nashwauk, despatched from Liverpool for Adelaide, South Australia; Irish Female Immigrants' Expenditure at Adelaide and Country Depots 1855–1856; Registered Cases of Destitution 1855–1856*; *The Minutes of Evidence of the Reports of the Select Committee of the Legislative Council of South Australia appointed to enquire into the Excessive Female Immigration; Adelaide Hospital Admission Register 1846–1871* – as well as general archival material. The passengers admitted to the Adelaide Hospital in the few weeks after the wreck were referred there by the Destitute Board, or the Colonial Surgeon. Alternative spellings of names are suggested as there were often problems with legibility in the documents.

Family connections were not indicated on the passenger list and so sibling relationships are only stated when confirmed with information from other sources. Common surnames have presented difficulties as in many cases relationships have remained unclear.

Ahearn, Catherine, 20, domestic servant, from Tipperary. Catholic. She left for Melbourne in the *Burra Burra* with a letter and cash from a brother in July 1855.

Barron, Mary, 22, domestic servant from Tipperary. Catholic. She was admitted to the Adelaide Hospital 28 May 1855 with 'febris' (fever) and discharged 13 July.

Birdy, Bridget, 19, farm servant from Clare. Catholic.

Blake (Bleake), Mary, 24, domestic servant from Limerick. Catholic. She was in the German Hospital and in the minutes of the Select Committee was recorded as having applied to go to Melbourne.

Brien, Johanna, 24, domestic servant from Carlow. Catholic. She was in the German Hospital. She went from the Clare Depot to Mrs Brydon as a servant on 24 August 1855.

Brien, Mary, 28, domestic servant from Tipperary. Catholic. She was in the German Hospital, and said she had applied to go to Melbourne when interviewed by Handasyde Duncan. She went to the Clare Depot and was engaged by Mrs Goldsmith of Watervale in September 1855 at 3/- a week.

Brooks, Mary, 18, domestic servant from Tipperary. Catholic. She was in the German Hospital, and was recorded as having applied to go to Melbourne.

Brody, Bridget, 19, domestic servant from Clare. Catholic. She was in the German Hospital.

Brophy, Bridget, 21, domestic servant from Kilkenny. Catholic. In the German Hospital. This name appears twice on the German Hospital list of June 1855, one Bridget applying for Melbourne, the other for Adelaide. However there is only one Bridget recorded on the *Nashwauk* passenger list!

Burke, Eliza, 23, domestic servant from Donegal, Free Church. She was in the German Hospital, where she said that she had applied to go to Melbourne.

Burke, Mary, 21, farm servant from Clare. Catholic. She was admitted to the Adelaide Hospital 1 June 1855 with 'febris' (fever) and discharged 6 July. In May 1856 a Mary Burke went to Port Adelaide by rail to go by ship to Port Lincoln as a servant for Captain Bishop.

Burns (Byrne), Mary, 20, farm servant from Cork. Catholic. She was in the German Hospital. She left for Melbourne in the *Havilah* in February 1856 with £10 cash and a letter from a cousin.

Butler (Batta), Catherine, 22, domestic servant, from Kilkenny. Catholic. She was in the German Hospital. A Catherine Butler left for McClaren Vale December 1855, on Simms and Co. transport.

Cahill, Mary, 19, farm servant, from Kilkenny. Catholic. In the German Hospital. She went from Adelaide to Auburn by Simms and Haines transport in November 1855 and was employed from the Clare Depot in August at 3/- a week by Mr Vi——? She is recorded as having applied to go to Sydney.

Caley, Margaret, 20, domestic servant, 'Irish'. Catholic. She was admitted to the Adelaide Hospital 28 May 1855 and discharged 28 June, having suffered 'febris' (fever). She was readmitted 13 August of the same year again with fever, and discharged 13 September, then recommended for relief by a Mr Thomas because she was convalescent.

Curless (Carlis, Curlis), Bridget, 23, domestic servant from Galway. Catholic. She was admitted to the Adelaide Hospital 28 May 1855 with 'febris' (fever) and discharged 13 July.

Carroll, Mary, 22, domestic servant from Tipperary. Catholic. She was admitted to the Adelaide Hospital 22 June 1855 with fever, and discharged 28 August.

Carthy, Catherine, 23, dairymaid from Tipperary. Catholic. She was in the German Hospital. She was employed from the Clare Depot, 30 August 1855, by Mrs Trezise, at 3/6 a week. She said she had applied to go to Melbourne.

Cash, Catherine 24, farm servant from Kings. Catholic. She was in the German Hospital, then from 26 July until 1 September 1855 was in the Adelaide Hospital with 'febris' (fever) and rheumatism. She said she had applied to go to Sydney.

Coffey (Coffee), Catherine, 20, servant from Kings. Catholic. She was in the German Hospital, and from the Clare Depot was engaged 27 July 1855 at 2/6 a week by Mr Hitchcock, saddler, Clare. A Catherine Coffey married Robert Henry of Armagh at Butler's residence June 1858.

Considine, Margaret, 19, farm servant from Clare. Catholic. She was in the German Hospital. She went to Kapunda from the Adelaide Depot in January 1856. She said she had applied to go to Melbourne.

Coppings, Mary, 31, farm servant from Galway. Catholic. She was in the German Hospital, and from the Clare Depot she was engaged in July 1855 at 2/6 a week by Mr Young, shepherd, Clare.

Cotter, Ellen (Mary), 22, farm servant from Cork. Catholic. She was in the German Hospital, and she said she had applied to go to Sydney.

Coughlan (Collins), Ellen, 27, domestic servant from Cork. Catholic. She was at the Clare Depot, and employed in September 1855 by Mr Rogers near Clare.

Crowley (Connelly), Ellen, 20, domestic servant, from Cork. Catholic. She was at the German Hospital, and she said she had applied to go to Melbourne. From the Clare Depot, she was employed in August 1855 at 2/6 a week, by Mr Blight from near Clare.

Collins (Cullens), Anastasia, 25, farm servant from Kilkenny. Catholic. From 29 May–14 August 1855 she was in the Adelaide Hospital with 'febris' (fever). She had applied for Melbourne and when interviewed by the Select Committee 1856 explained that her parents were not happy when she boarded the ship for Adelaide but were told 'by the person they paid money to' it was easy to get to Melbourne from Adelaide. She had no friend on board, but friends in Melbourne. She had spent three weeks in the Adelaide Depot by February 1856.

Curtain, Eliza, 24, servant from Cork. Catholic.

Dalton, Ellen, 21, domestic servant from Tipperary. Catholic. She was in the German Hospital. She was sent to the Clare Depot, and engaged 31 July 1855 at 2/6 a week by Mrs Frankzism of Macklin (?) She said she had applied to go to Melbourne.

Dempsey, Fanny, 19, farm servant from Tipperary. Catholic. She was in the German Hospital. She said she had applied to go to Melbourne.

Devlin, Rose, 18, domestic servant from Derry. Catholic. She was in the Clare Depot and employed by Mrs Rowe of Clare in August 1855 at 2/6 a week. A Hugh Devlin 19, from Derry who was also a passenger, and a Cook's assistant was probably her brother.

Dineen (De Neill), Allie, 19, domestic servant from Tipperary. Catholic. She was in the German Hospital, and paid £2 as a sub matron on the ship.

Donahue, Mary, 20, domestic servant, seamstress, from Limerick. Catholic. She was in the German Hospital.

Donahue, Ellen, 15, domestic servant from Limerick. Catholic. In the German Hospital.

Donovan, Eliza (Bessie), 22, dairymaid from Cork. Catholic. She was in the German Hospital. She was employed from the Clare Depot in August 1855, by Mrs Rowe of Clare, at 2/6 a week.

Doughney, Honora, 30, domestic servant from Lancaster. Church of England. Nurse on board ship, paid £2.

Doyle, Catherine, 21, domestic servant from Limerick. Catholic. C. Doyle went to Horseshoe Bay December 1855, via Simms and Co. The death of a Catherine Doyle is recorded in the Death Register on 11 June 1856.

Dwyer, Mary, 20, domestic servant from Tipperary. Catholic. She said she had applied to go to Melbourne.

Digedan (Dyson, Diggedan, Degan), Bridget, 20, farm servant, from Clare. Catholic. She was admitted to the Adelaide Hospital on 24 May 1855 and discharged 21 June, condition 'febris' (fever).

Digedan, Margaret, 16, farm servant from Clare. Catholic. She was in the German Hospital. These girls may have been sisters, as both said they had applied to go to Melbourne.

Feighney, Bridget, 22, domestic servant from Clare. Catholic. She was ill after the wreck.

Fennelly, Catherine, 17, domestic servant from Tipperary. Catholic. She was recorded as being in the Destitute Asylum soon after the wreck.

Fernie, Eliza, 32, domestic servant from Lancaster. Church of England. She was sub matron and paid £2 on the ship. She was employed by Mr E.S. Wigg of Adelaide after the wreck, but first nursed the sick passengers.

Fitzgerald, Judith (Joanna), 32, farm servant from Tipperary. Catholic. In the German Hospital.

Fitzgerald, Margaret, 24, farm servant from Tipperary. Catholic. In the German Hospital. From the Clare Depot she was engaged in August 1855 at 2/6 a week by Mr Diarwood of Amargh near Clare.

Flaherty, Bridget, 22, domestic servant from Clare. Catholic. She was employed from the Clare Depot in August 1855 by Mrs Ashley, from near Clare, at 2/6 a week.

Flynn, Catherine, 23, domestic servant from Cork. Catholic.

Foggarty (Fogerty), Ann, 21, domestic servant from Tipperary. Catholic. She was in the German Hospital. From the Clare Depot she was engaged in July 1855 at 2/6 a week, by Mr Robinson, from near Clare.

Foggarty, Mary, 19, domestic servant from Tipperary. Catholic. She was in the German Hospital. She said she had applied to go to Melbourne. From the Clare Depot she was engaged in July 1855 by Mr Gleeson, gentleman, of Clare.

Green, Margaret, 20, domestic servant from Clare. Catholic. From the Clare Depot she was engaged in August 1855 at 2/6 a week by Mrs Craig of Clare.

Gavan, Margaret, 18, domestic servant from Tipperary. Catholic. On 30 November 1855 she went to Auburn from Adelaide Depot on Simms and Co.

Gorman, Anne, 28, domestic servant from Carlow. Catholic. She was in the German Hospital.

Hanlon (Hanlan), Catherine, 19, domestic servant from Westmeath, Catholic, placed in the German Hospital. She went to Melbourne with a letter and cash from an Uncle in July 1855.

Hanlon, Mary, 20, domestic servant from Westmeath. Catholic. She was at the German Hospital.

Healy, Margaret, 19, domestic servant and farm servant from Cork. Catholic. She was in the German Hospital. She went from Adelaide to a situation in Kapunda in December 1855. She was interviewed by the Select Committee, where she said she had applied to go to Melbourne.

Heffernan, Mary, 20, farm servant from Clare. Catholic. She was at the German Hospital.

Hehir (Hare), Mary, 25, dairymaid from Clare. Catholic. She was at the German Hospital. She said she had applied to go to Melbourne.

Hennessy, Catherine (Mary), 20, domestic servant from Clare. Catholic. She was at the German Hospital. She said she had applied to go to Melbourne. She was employed from the Clare Depot on the 24 August 1855 by Mrs Johnson, of White Water, at 2/6 a week.

Heydon, Anne, 22, domestic servant from Carlow. Catholic. Honor Heydon was employed from Willunga Depot at 4/- a week in November 1855.

Hinchen (Inchen), Bridget, 19, domestic servant from Cork. Catholic. She was at the German Hospital. She was admitted to the Adelaide Hospital 3 November 1855 and discharged 5 January 1856, after 'morbi oculorum' (diseased eyes).

Hoar (Hare, Hoare), Alice, 19, domestic servant from Tipperary. Catholic. Placed at the German Hospital. She said that she had applied for Sydney. Alice was in the Adelaide Depot at the time the Select Committee was meeting. She had been admitted to the Adelaide Hospital on 15 January 1856 and discharged on 6 February, suffering from 'rheumatismus' (rheumatism).

Hoar, Margaret, 23, domestic servant from Tipperary. Catholic. She was in the German Hospital.

Hoare (Hoar), Bridget, 22, laundress from Clare. Catholic. In the German Hospital.

Houlihan, Hannah, 18, domestic servant from Cork. Catholic. An Ann Houlihan (Hourigan) was at the German Hospital.

Hourigan, Lucy, 23, domestic servant from Limerick. Catholic. She was a hospital assistant on the ship, and paid £3. She was at the Clare Depot and was employed by Mr Harrison of Clare at 2/6 a week, on 30 July 1855.

Ines (Jones), Ann, 23, domestic servant from Clare. Catholic. In the German Hospital she said she had applied to go to Melbourne. She was engaged from Clare Depot August 1855 at 3/6 a week by Mr Wood, of Penwortham.

Ivory, Margaret, 26, farm servant from Kilkenny. Catholic. She was at the German Hospital.

Keally, Margaret, 25, farm servant from Kilkenny. Catholic. She left for Melbourne with a letter and £7 from an uncle, on the *Havilah* in October 1855.

Kennedy, Mary, 19, farm servant from Kings. Catholic. At the German Hospital. She said she had applied to go to Melbourne.

Keating, Eliza (Elizabeth), 19, farm servant from Cork. Catholic. She spent from 23 May until 31 July 1855 in the Adelaide Hospital with 'febris' (fever). She left for Melbourne on the *Havilah* October 1855.

Kiely, Honora, 20, domestic servant from Cork. Catholic.

Kelleher (Kelcher, Callaghan), Bridget, 20, domestic servant from Clare. Catholic. She was at the German Hospital. She had applied to go to Sydney. From the Clare Depot she was employed at 5/- a week by Mrs Paech of Penwortham, in August 1855.

Kelcher **(Kelleher),** Susan, 19, sister of Bridget. Catholic. Employed from the Clare Depot by Mr Bryden who lived near Skillolagee Creek, at 5/- a week, in September 1855. She married Edward Nicholls of Skillolagee Creek 13 January 1856, at Clare.

Kelly, Ellen, 26, domestic servant from Tipperary. Catholic. In the German Hospital. She said she applied to go to Melbourne.

Kelly, Honora, 20, domestic servant from Tipperary. Catholic. In the German Hospital.

Kelly, Bridget, 17, farm servant, from Ireland. Catholic. Recommended for relief by Mrs Abins after working for three weeks, then 'out of place'. Address Bowden.

Keaire, (Kerin, Keaire), Mary, 21, domestic servant from Clare, Catholic.

Kennedy, Bridget, 24, domestic servant from Tipperary. Catholic. She was in the German Hospital and said she had applied to go to Sydney.

Lally (Luby), Ellen, 20, domestic servant from Tipperary. Catholic. In the German Hospital she said she had applied for Sydney. From the Clare Depot she was employed in August 1855 at 3/- a week by Mr Beard of Penwortham.

Leahy (Lahey), Bridget, 17, domestic servant from Tipperary. Catholic. In the German Hospital she said she had applied to go to Sydney, and left in June 1856 with a letter and shipping order from an aunt, on the *White Swan.*

Leary (O'Leary), Johannah, 20, domestic servant from Cork. Catholic. At the German Hospital. From the Clare Depot she was employed in September 1855 at 3/- a week by Mr Paul Tierzk? from near Wakefield. She married Robert Giles of Kooringa, 10 June 1856.

Leary, Mary, 32, domestic servant from Cork, Catholic, recommended for relief by Mr Regan after leaving a situation at Mud Hut because of problems with her hands. In September 1855 she was in the Destitute Asylum.

Lonigan, Ellen, 23, farm servant from Kilkenny. Catholic. In July 1855 she had left employment and was without means, address Norwood. She applied for relief July 1855.

Loughman (Lokeman, Loakman), Mary, 26, domestic servant from Tipperary. At the German Hospital. From the Clare Depot she was employed in August 1855 at 2/6 a week by Mrs Slater (?) near Clare.

Mackrell, Sarah, 20, seamstress from Londonderry. Irish Protestant. She applied for relief August 1855, as she was out of work, and destitute, residing at the Port.

McDonald, Ellen 19, domestic servant from Cork. Catholic. At the German Hospital. She said she had applied to go to Melbourne. From the Clare Depot she was engaged at 2/6 a week by Mr Spratt, blacksmith, of Clare, in July 1855. From here she was sent away by mail coach because she 'got too close to Spratt' in January 1856. An Ellen McDonald married Thomas Edmunds of Kooringa at St Joseph's Church 13 December 1857. A baby, Frances, was born in September 1860 (SA Births, Index of Registrations 1842–1906).

Magree, Bridget, 29, domestic servant from Kilkenny. Catholic. Sub matron on the ship and paid £2. She was in the German Hospital. She went to Melbourne on the *White Swan* in June 1856.

Magree, Bessie (Elizabeth), 22, domestic servant from Kilkenny. Sister of Bridget. Also in the German Hospital, and had applied to go to Melbourne. They both paid their own way there on the *White Swan* in June 1856.

Maher (Mahir, Minahar), Bridget, 26, domestic servant from Tipperary. Catholic. She spent from 2 June until 22 June 1855 in the Adelaide Hospital, with 'febris' (fever). She had applied for Melbourne and left on the *White Swan* in June 1856.

Malony (Malone), Eliza, 18, domestic servant from Kings. Catholic.

Malone, Judy, 20, domestic servant from Kilkenny. Catholic.

McCarty, Honorah, 21, dairymaid from Cork. Catholic. She was in the German Hospital and was engaged from the Clare Depot by Mr Mc Waters in August 1855 at 4/- a week.

McCaughey (McCarthy), Margaret, 22, domestic servant from Londonderry. Catholic. She was admitted to the Adelaide Hospital 1 June 1855 with 'febris' (fever) and discharged 12 July.

McDougall (McDowall), Mary, 20, domestic servant, from Donegal. Church of England. She was in the German Hospital, and paid her own passage to Melbourne in December 1855 aboard the *White Swan.* She had a letter from a cousin.

McLaughlin (McGlaughlin), Mary, 18, domestic servant from Donegal. Catholic. She was in the German Hospital and said she had applied to go to Melbourne.

McManus, Catherine, 22, farm servant from Fermagh. Catholic. She was in the German Hospital. She complained of the neglect of the Ship's Surgeon. She said she had applied to go to Sydney

McNamara, Anne, 22, farm servant from Clare. Catholic.

McPeake, Anne, 19, domestic servant from Londonderry. Catholic.

Minihan, Bridget, 18, farm servant from Clare. Catholic. In the German Hospital she said she had applied to go to Melbourne. From the Clare Depot she was engaged in September 1855 at 2/- a week, by Mr Thomas of Auburn.

Moore, Margaret, 20, domestic servant from Kings. Catholic. In the German Hospital. She was admitted to the Adelaide Hospital 28 May and not discharged until 19 July 1855, after suffering 'febris' (fever). She had applied to go to Sydney.

Moore, Ellen, 20, domestic servant from Kings. Catholic. In the German Hospital. She said she had applied to go to Melbourne. From the Clare Depot she was engaged July 1855 at 2/6 a week by Mrs McKenzie, inn keeper, of Clare.

Morton (Moran, Mooran), Mary, 22, needle woman from Limerick. Catholic. In the German Hospital she said she had applied to go to Sydney.

Moylan, Ann, 22, farm servant from Tipperary. Catholic.

Mulcahy (Muleahy), Abigail (Aby), 19, domestic servant from Cork. Catholic. In the German Hospital. She had applied for Melbourne, and left in February 1856 on the *Havilah* with a letter and cash from a cousin.

Murphy, Hannah, 19, domestic servant from Cork. Catholic. In the German Hospital. She said she had applied to go to Melbourne.

Murphy, Mary, 26, domestic servant from Cork. Catholic. In the German Hospital. She said she had applied to go to Melbourne.

Murphy, Mary, 20, domestic servant from Kilkenny. Catholic. In the German Hospital. She said she had applied to go to Melbourne.

Nally, Mary, 22, domestic servant from Galway. Catholic. In the German Hospital she said she had applied to go to Melbourne.

Neal (O'Niel), Honora (Hannah, Ann), 23, domestic servant from Tipperary. Catholic. In the German Hospital. From the Clare Depot, she was engaged at 2/6 a week by Mrs Goldsmith, of Watervale.

Nunan (Nonan), Bridget, 20, farm servant from Clare. Catholic. In the German Hospital. She said she had applied to go to Sydney. From the Clare Depot in September 1855 she was employed at 3/- a week by Mr I——? from near Clare.

O'Brien, Bridget, 22, farm servant from Clare. Catholic. In the German Hospital. From the Clare Depot she was employed by Mrs Burscott near Clare (Armagh) in August 1855, at 2/6 a week. She married Benjamin Horne. A daughter, Ellen, was born in 1859. George and other children were subsequently born at Auburn.

O'Brien, Catherine, 20, laundress from Clare. Catholic.

O'Shea, Bridget, 20, domestic servant from Limerick. Catholic. In the German Hospital. She said she had applied to go to Sydney.

Piper (Pigot, Pearce), Mary, 19, domestic servant from Tipperary. Catholic. In the German Hospital. She said she had applied to go to Melbourne. She went to the Clare Depot.

Purcell, Margaret, 22, domestic servant from Galway. Catholic. In the German Hospital she said she had applied to go to Sydney.

Randell, Jane, 24, domestic servant from Dublin. Catholic. The Ship's Surgeon complained that she flirted with the Captain on the ship (Ship's Papers). In May 1856 she was conveyed from the Adelaide Depot to Horse Shoe Bay.

Riordan (Redling, Reardon), Bridget (Bridgid), 20, domestic servant from Cork. Catholic. In the German Hospital she said she had applied for Melbourne. She fell overboard from the *Melbourne* when a deck rail gave way close to Pt Noarlunga. She was rescued possibly by Jacob Haarsma whom she later married. She went to the Clare Depot and was employed by Mr Rogers, school teacher. After marriage to Jacob Haarsma she lived at Seven Hills, and had nine children.

Roney, Mary, 25, domestic servant from Galway. Catholic. In the German Hospital.

Ready (Reedy), Mary, 28, domestic servant from Limerick. Catholic. She was in the German Hospital, then resided at Glenelg. From September 1855 she received indoor relief because she was out of work. December 1855 a Mary Ready was transported to Kapunda from the Adelaide Depot.

Riley (Byall), Mary, 23, farm servant from Cork. Catholic. Though not on the original passenger list her name appears when she was interviewed by the Select Committee, where she explained that she had been sick for five months after arriving. She claimed that she had applied for Sydney as she had cousins there doing well. She boarded the *Nashwauk* bound for Adelaide because she was told there was no vessel sailing to Sydney and the *Nashwauk* did not have enough passengers. She had always lived at home in the country, and had milked, washed, and worked in the house. She had never been in service. She was without friends, and since being well had found no work. She had not been in a country depot.

Ryal (Ryan), Catherine, 25, domestic servant from Cork. Catholic. In the German Hospital. She said she had applied to go to Melbourne. From the Clare Depot in August 1855 she was employed by Mr Horrocks of Penwortham at 3/- a week.

Ryal, Mary, 23, domestic servant, from Cork. Catholic. From the Clare Depot she was employed in August 1855 by Mr Hope of Clare, at 3/- a week. Mr Hope was the Manager of Bungaree.

Roney (Roony), Mary, 25, domestic servant from Galway. Catholic, and in the German Hospital.

Ryan, Bridget, 19, domestic servant from Tipperary. In the German Hospital she claimed she had applied to go to Sydney.

Ryan Bridget, 24, dairymaid from Tipperary. Catholic. In the German Hospital. From the Clare Depot she was engaged in August 1855 at 2/6 a week by Mrs Frankzism.

Ryan, Catherine, 20, domestic servant from Tipperary. Catholic. In the German Hospital. She said she had applied to go to Melbourne. She was transported from the Adelaide Depot in March 1856 to Burra for Mr Cooper.

Ryan, Ellen, 25, dairymaid from Tipperary. Catholic. In the German Hospital. She left for Melbourne on the *White Swan* in June 1856 with an order and the shipping cost from an aunt.

Ryan, Judith, 20, farm servant from Tipperary. Catholic. In the German Hospital she said she had applied to go to Melbourne.

Ryan, Margaret, domestic servant, from Tipperary. Catholic. There were two Margaret Ryans, from Tipperary listed as passengers on the *Nashwauk*, one aged 25, the other 22, only one recorded as staying at the German Hospital. Because the name is common and details are confusing it is not possible to establish which Margaret was in the German Hospital, or even which ones were *Nashwauk* passengers! A Margaret Ryan was in court at Port Adelaide in January 1856 because she had stolen £13 and some silver from Mr Robinson, of Salisbury, when she was a servant. She was not committed to gaol. Presumably the same Margaret Ryan was again on trial for larceny in October 1856 when she stole gloves and three handkerchiefs from Martha Porter of Adelaide, when she was a servant for Porter. The property was returned. A Margaret Ryan applied for relief in September 1855, her residence then given as Grenfell St. She had lost her job, because of 'conduct immoral'. One Margaret Ryan was listed at the Clare Depot at the end of 1855 and in March 1856 was returned to Adelaide by order of Mr Gleeson, after medical attention for three weeks. Perhaps this Margaret, residing in South Terrace, in October 1856 again applied for relief because she had a bad breast and was given indoor relief, recommended by Dr Gosse. She had no friends and a bad foot. A Margaret Ryan, age given as 19, who was identified as a passenger on the *Nashwauk* (although none was listed as being 19) was committed to the Lunatic Asylum by Dr Gosse early in 1856 as an "imbecile." The reason given is social dislocation due to the trauma of immigration. Perhaps this was the Margaret

Ryan who was put into handcuffs (irons) on the ship for unruly behaviour. The history of the two Margaret Ryans from Tipperary is impossible to determine accurately.

Ryan, Mary, 20, domestic servant from Kings. Catholic. In the German Hospital. She was recommended for relief in July 1855, by Mrs Alford of the Stag Inn in Rundle Street, as she was 'inefficient and immoral' and therefore out of work.

Ryan, Joanna, 22, domestic servant from Limerick. Catholic. In the German Hospital. From the Clare Depot she was employed 24 August 1855 by Mrs Brydon near Clare.

Saxby, Sarah, 27, cook from Dublin. Catholic. From September 1855 she was unable to work because of a bad arm. She was allowed to remain with her employer, Mrs Philips of Port Adelaide, and receive relief.

Seaton (Sexton), Mary, 19, domestic servant from Clare. Catholic. In the German Hospital. From the Clare Depot, she was engaged in September 1855 at 3/- a week by Mr Brady, from near Clare.

Shea (Sheer), Judith, 19, domestic servant from Kilkenny. Catholic. In the German Hospital she said she had applied to go to Sydney.

Shea, Mary, 22, domestic servant from Kilkenny. Catholic. In the German Hospital.

Sheehan, Anne, 21, domestic servant from Cork. Catholic. In the German Hospital she said she had applied to go to Melbourne. She was admitted to the Adelaide Hospital 29 August and died 30 September 1855 of 'psithis' (TB).

Simmon, Mary, 20, domestic servant from Carlow. Catholic. In the German Hospital. She said she had applied to go to Melbourne.

Sinnot, Ellen, 25, farm servant from Kilkenny. Catholic. She worked first for Mr Haster and proved unsuitable by September. Then she worked for Mr Gowan, and again was unsuitable. From a residence in Norwood she applied for relief in December 1855.

Speer, Mary, 27, domestic servant from Doncaster. Catholic.

Slattery, Nancy, 22, domestic servant from Tipperary. Catholic. In the German Hospital she said she had applied to go to Melbourne. From the Clare Depot, in September 1855 she was engaged at 3/- a week by Mr Freeman of Clare.

Stanley, Catherine, 23, domestic servant from Kilkenny. Catholic. She was admitted to the Adelaide Hospital on 17 May and died 22 May 1855 from 'febris' (fever).

Stanley, Catherine, 20, from Kilkenny. Catholic. Recorded at the German Hospital.

Storan, Ellen, 20, domestic servant from Clare. Catholic. In the German Hospital she said she had applied to go to Melbourne. She was suffering from 'morbi oculorum' (diseased eyes) and was referred by Mr Ennis from the Adelaide Depot to the Adelaide Hospital on 15 October 1855. She was discharged on 24 January 1856 and was recommended for relief by Dr Thomas because she was convalescent.

Stapleton, Alley, 28, domestic servant from Tipperary. Catholic. In the German Hospital. She left for Melbourne on the *White Swan* October 1855 with letter and cash, from a cousin.

Sullivan, Lucy, 23, domestic servant from Dublin. Catholic. In the German Hospital.

Sweetman, Catherine (Anne), 23, farm servant from Tipperary. Catholic. In the German Hospital she said she had applied to go to Melbourne.

Sweetman, Margaret, 18, domestic servant from Tipperary. Catholic. In the German Hospital she also said she had applied for Melbourne.

Toole, Mary, 18, housemaid from Clare. Catholic. In the German Hospital she said she had applied to go to Melbourne.

Treacy (Tracey), Honora, 22, dairymaid from Tipperary. Catholic. She spent 28 May to the 28 June 1855 in the Adelaide Hospital with 'febris' (fever). She then went to the Clare Depot and was employed by Mr Taylor Watervale at 3/- a week in August 1855.

Wall, Catherine, 20, farm servant from Kilkenny. Catholic. In the German Hospital.

Walsh, Mary, 23, domestic servant from Kilkenny. Catholic. In the German Hospital. From Adelaide transport to MacCaw Creek is recorded in December 1855.

Walsh, Mary, 22, domestic servant from Clare. Catholic. She said she had applied for Sydney but in fact she left for Melbourne with a letter and cash from a sister, on the *Havilah* in October 1855.

Watson, Ellen, domestic servant, had applied for Melbourne and had no relatives or friends in the colony. Though not recorded in the passenger list, she was interviewed by the Select Committee and identified as a passenger on the *Nashwauk*

Whelan, Ellen, 26, domestic servant from Tipperary. Catholic. She was paid £2 as a sub matron on the ship. In the German Hospital she said she had applied for Sydney. She had no relatives or friends in South Australia.

Whelan, Judith, 28, domestic servant from Tipperary. Catholic. In the German Hospital she also said she had applied for Sydney.

Whelan, Catherine, 23, farm servant from Tipperary. Catholic. In the German Hospital. She was employed from the Clare Depot in August 1855 at 2/6 a week by Mr Diarwood (?) from near Clare.

Whelan, Mathilda, 20, domestic servant from Clare, Catholic.

White, Bridget, 24, domestic servant from Clare. Catholic. In the German Hospital. She was engaged in September 1855 at 3/- a week by Mr Evans of Auburn. A Bridget White married John Coussin of Bungaree 7 May 1856.

White, Bridget, 22, domestic servant from Galway. Catholic. In the German Hospital. From the Clare Depot she was engaged in August 1855 at 4/- a week by Mr Beacon near Broughton.

Whitfield, Alicia, 20, farm servant from Kings. Catholic. She applied for relief June 1856, with a bad hand, unfit for work and destitute, residing at the Bay.

Woods, Ellen, 28, farm servant from Clare. Catholic. In the German Hospital.

Woods, Ellen, 18, dairymaid from Kilkenny. Catholic. In the German Hospital. From the Clare Depot, one Ellen Woods was engaged at 3/6 a week by Mr Richmond, of Clare.

APPENDIX TWO

Statistics

The number of girls at the depot, 8 October 1855: 640
Admitted since from on board ship: 648
Readmitted by Board: 960
TOTAL: 2248

The number who left the depot for service: 1672
The number remaining in the depot: 25
The number placed from country depots: 451
TOTAL: 2248

The number of girls refused admission or dismissed for refusing to take situations or other misconduct: 153
(GRG CSO 24/6/1856/1459)

Number of females sent from the central depot to each country depot by 28 January 1856:

Clare: 121
Willunga: 61
Guichen Bay: 80 (including Penola and Mount Gambier)
Encounter Bay: 91
Gawler: 129
Mount Barker: 246

In addition areas without depots were included
Morphett Vale: 12
Yankalilla: 17

APPENDIX THREE

Colonial Secretary's Letter

Colonial Secretary's Office, Adelaide,
June 27, 1855

Sir-

I am desired by His Excellency the Governor-in-Chief to state, for the information of yourself and the District Council of [blank] that there are at present in the Colony several hundreds of single females--immigrants from Ireland-- about the disposal of whom some difficulty is experienced-- as neither at Adelaide, nor in its immediate neighborhood, is there at present any further demand for that class of immigrant.

2. Many of those females are highly respectable, and well qualified as in-door domestic servants; but the majority of them have not yet acquired experience sufficient to render them immediately useful in that capacity. They are, however, strong, healthy, and willing to be employed as farm servants, having, most of them, already served in that capacity.

3. It appears to His Excellency, that in the towns and agricultural districts of the Colony, there must be employment for many hundreds of industrious females of the class last described; and that their services might be immediately and usefully rendered available, if the parties willing to engage them could do so without the expense and inconvenience of a journey to Adelaide.

4. It is, therefore, the object of His Excellency to place those who are willing to give employment, and those who are ready to be employed, in closer proximity to one another, that both parties may conveniently enter into arrangements mutually beneficial.

5. It is, therefore, intended to classify the immigrants in question, as far as practicable, dividing them into two classes--first, domestic servants; and secondly, farm laborers. His Excellency has also determined that, where the circumstances may admit of his doing so, he will endeavor to find the means of transport for the immigrants in question to those places where there may appear to be a sufficient demand for their services; pecuniary remuneration--suitable board, lodging, and clothing being, for the present, considered an equivalent for their services; it would, however, be for the District Council of [blank] to say how long such temporary arrangement ought to be expected to last, in fairness to both parties.

6. I am, therefore, instructed to request that you, and the district Council of [blank] will, as soon as possible, take into your consideration, and forward to me replies to, the following questions, which involve the most material points to be determined in the first instance:–

1st. What demand exists in the District of [blank] for female domestics, or female farm servants, of the class above indicated?

2nd. Would any, and what, advantages attend the establishment of a Depot for female immigrants, and for what number of such immigrants in the District of [blank] or its neighborhood; those immigrants being boarded and lodged in such Depot whilst waiting employment?

3rd. Supposing the establishment of such Depot expedient, what facilities does the District of [blank] afford for its erection and maintenance, and what would be the probable cost per diem of rationing each female immigrant?

4th. Are there any, and what, buildings to be hired in the said District suitable to the purposes of such Depot, and if so at what rate? And

5th. Are there any and what parties in the said District willing to contact for the maintenance in the said Depot of the females who might be sent there?

7. On receiving replies to the foregoing questions, His Excellency will be prepared, when practicable, to convey to the District Council of [blank] as many female immigrants as they may be of opinion are likely to find employment there; and he entirely relies on the Council using a sound and careful discretion in recommending none but suitable parties as employers of female labor.

8. I am further desired to state that His Excellency considers the difficulty occasioned by the arrival of so many female immigrants at this unseasonable period of the year to be precisely that species of difficulty in which the Executive may fairly expect to be aided by the local experience and public spirit of the respective District Councils. You will, however, observe, that the value of each assistance will be greatly enhanced by its being afforded speedily; and, therefore, His Excellency requests that the information asked for above may be furnished by the first possible opportunity.

I have the honor to be,

Sir,

Your obedient servant,

Colonial Secretary.

BIBLIOGRAPHY

Primary Sources

Adelaide City Council, Assessment Books, 4th series 534, vol. 2, 1855.

Adelaide Catholic Archives, Mount Barker Mission, Register of Births and Baptisms, 1848–1880

Adelaide Catholic Archives, Sevenhills, Register of Marriages, 1849–1858

Adelaide Catholic Archives, Father Michael Ryan, box 36

Mortlock Library, Temme Index of South Australian Shipwrecks, 1853–1855

Noarlunga Library, Local History Collection

South Australia, Parliament, papers:

Legislative Council of South Australia, paper 66, Wreck of the *Nashwauk*, 4 December 1855

Legislative Council of South Australia, paper 137, Report of the Select Committee appointed to inquire into Excessive Female Immigration; together with Minutes of Evidence and Appendix, 7 March 1856

Legislative Council of South Australia, paper 95, Female Immigrant Depot, 23 January 1856

Legislative Council of South Australia, Willunga Immigration Depot, 24 January 1856

South Australia, Chief Secretary's Office, Statistical Register of South Australia, Adelaide, Government Printer, 1860–1875

South Australia, Colonial Secretary's Office, Blue Book of South Australia, Statistical returns prepared for the Colonial Secretary's Office, 1839–1866

South Australia, Births, Deaths and Marriages Registration Division, Indexes to Birth, Deaths and Marriage Records 1842–1906, microfiche

South Australian Government Gazette, 1855, 1856

State Records of South Australia,

Australian Joint Copying Project, Colonial Office, 13/90, 1855, Classified Return of Irish Female Immigrants supported by Government, 27 June 1855

General Records Group, 24/6, 1855, no. 1828, Trinity Board Enquiry

General Records Group, 28/1/2, letter book, 1855–1856

General Records Group, 28/4, 1855–1856, Registered Cases of Destitution

General Records Group, 35/48A, 1855, Nominal List of Emigrants on board the *Nashwauk* dispatched from Liverpool for Adelaide, South Australia.

General Records Group, 35/48, 1855, Persons Entitled to Gratuities for Services Performed on Board the Emigrant Ship *Nashwauk*

General Records Group, 35/301, Irish Female Immigration, Expenditure at Adelaide and Country depots, 1855–1856

Research Notes, vol. 5, No. 236, Irish women Immigrants and Highlanders families who were sent to Robe in 1855

Municipal Records Group, 43/1, Mount Barker District Council Minutes, 1855

Municipal Records Group, 24/1, Mudla Wirra District Council Minutes, 1855

United Kingdom, Westminster, South Australian Government Immigration Office, Regulations for Selection of Emigrants and Conditions to which Passages are granted to South Australia, no. 31, October 1854

Newspapers

Adelaide Observer

Adelaide Times

Advertiser

Mail

South Australian Register

South Australian Gazette and Colonial Register

Unpublished Works

Baker, Penelope, 'The Position of Women in South Australia 1836-76', BA Thesis, University of Adelaide, 1977

Bettison, I.J., 'Kapunda', BA Thesis, University of Adelaide, 1960

Campbell, Sue, 'Women and Law in SA 1836–1936', BA Thesis, University of Adelaide, 1975

Fitzgerald, S.H., 'Half a World Away: South Australian Migration 1857–72', BA Thesis, University of Adelaide, 1969

Grainger, Geoffrey, 'Matthew Moorhouse and the South Australian Aborigines 1839–1856', BA Thesis, Flinders University, 1980

Haines, Robin, 'Government Assisted Immigration from the United Kingdom to Australia 1831–1860: Promotion, Recruitment and the Labouring Poor', PhD Thesis, Flinders University, 1992

Herriman, A., 'Irish Girls Defend Their Honour and Their Rights', Paper presented to the Historical Society of South Australia, 2 July 1999

Herriman, A., 'Irish Settlers beyond the Tiers, Mount Barker, South Australia 1836-1886', unpublished abstract

Horan, S., 'More Sinned Against than Sinning: Prostitution in South Australia, 1836–1914', BA Thesis, Flinders University, 1978

McClean, Christopher, 'Dr Handasyde Duncan as Immigration Agent in SA: 1853–1878', BA Thesis, Flinders University, 1992

Millburn, Elizabeth, 'Clare, 1840–1900', MA Thesis, University of Adelaide, 1982

Parkin, C.W., 'Irish Female Immigration to South Australia during the Great Famine', BA Thesis, University of Adelaide, 1964

Secondary Sources

Bermingham, Kathleen, *Gateway to the South East*, South East Times, Millicent, 1961

Blackett, John, *The Early History of South Australia*, Vandon & Sons, Adelaide, 1907

Branson, Joyce, *Pioneer Pastor of the South: Life and Work of Rev. Ridgway William Newland, 1790–1864*, J. Branson, Victor Harbor, 1989

Branson, V.M., *Clare and District Sketchbook: Drawings by Arthur Phillips*, Rigby, Adelaide, 1975

Callen, Janet, *What Really Happened to the* Nashwauk*?*, Callen, Blackwood, 2004

Cameron, John, *A Band of Pioneers*, Central Times, Adelaide, 1977

Charlton, Robert, *The History of Kapunda*, Hawthorn Press, Melbourne, 1971

Colwell, Max and Naylor, Alan, *Adelaide: An Illustrated History*, Landsdowne Press, Adelaide, 1974

Coombe, E.H., *History of Gawler 1837–1908*, facsimile, Gawler Institute, 1978

Dickey, B., *Rations, Residence, Resources*, Wakefield Press, Adelaide, 1986

Dunn, J., *A Miller's Tale*, ed. Anthony Stuart, Waterwheel Books, Kingswood, 1991

Dunstan, Martin, *Willunga; Town and District, 1837–1900*, Lynton Publications, Blackwood, 1977

Fowler, David J., *A Fortunate Locality. A History of Noarlunga and District*, Peacock Publications, Adelaide, 1986

Garran, Andrew, ed., *The Royal South Australian Almanack and General Directory*, Register & Observer, Adelaide, 1855

Geyer, Mary, *Behind the Walls: The Women of the Destitute Asylum, 1852–1918*, Axiom Publishing, Adelaide, 1994

Gibbs, R.M., *A History of South Australia*, Southern Heritage, Mitcham, 1999

Hall, Henry, *The Colonial Office: A History*, Longmans, Green and Co., London, 1937

Harcus, William, ed., *South Australia: Its History, Resources and Productions*, Cox, Adelaide, 1876

Harmstorf, Ian, 'True Germans are Patriotic South Australian. South Australian Germans before 1918', Historical Society of South Australia, journal 17, 1989

Hawker, F. and Linn, R., *Bungaree, Land, Stock and People*, Turnbull Fox Phillips, Adelaide, 1992

Hodder, E., *The History of South Australia*, Sampson Low, Marston & Co., London, 1893

Hodge, Charles R., *Encounter Bay: The Miniature Naples of South Australia*, C. Hodge, Adelaide, 1932

Hughes, J. Escourt, *A History of the Royal Adelaide Hospital*, RAH Board of Management, Adelaide, 1967

Ingpen, Robert, *Robe: A Portrait of the Past*, Rigby, Adelaide, 1975

Jones, H., *In Her Own Name: Women in South Australian History*, Wakefield Press, Adelaide, 1986

Johnson, Win., *Cottages and Cameos of Clare*, Clare District Council, 1988

Kapunda District Council, *Kapunda. Centenary Celebrations, 1946*

Laube, Anthony, *Settlers Around the Bay: The Pioneering Families of Encounter Bay and Victor Harbor*, Laube, Adelaide, 1985

Linn, R., *Cradle of Adversity: A History of the Willunga District*, Historical Consultants, Blackwood, 1991

Loyau, George, *The Gawler Handbook including the memoirs of Dr Nott*, Adelaide, Goodfellow & Hele, 1880

Loyau, George, *The Representative Men of South Australia*, G. Howell, Adelaide, 1883

Martin, Vivien, *Mostly Mount Barker*, Martin, Adelaide, 1982

McClaughlin, T., *Barefoot and Pregnant?: Irish Famine orphans in Australia, documents and register compiled and introduced by Trevor McClaughlin*, Genealogy Society of Victoria, Melbourne, c. 1991

Mount Barker District Council, *Mount Barker Heritage Walk, 1992*

Nance, Christopher, 'The Irish in SA during the Colony's first four decades', Historical Society of South Australia, journal 5, 1978

Nance, Christopher, 'Making a Better Society?: Immigration to South Australia, 1936–1871', Historical Society of South Australia, journal 12, 1984

Noye, Robert J., *Clare: A District History*, Lynton Publications, Coromandel Valley, 1975

Newland, Simpson, *A Band of pioneers*, Hassell & Son, Adelaide, 1919

Parham, D., *Architecture of the Destitute Asylum*, Flinders University Art Museum, Adelaide, 1983

Parsons, Ronald, *Migrant Ships for South Australia, 1836–1860*, Wakefield Press, Adelaide, 1988

Piddoch, Susan, *Accommodating the Destitute*, Flinders University, Adelaide, 1996

Pike, D., *Australian Dictionary of Biography*, Melbourne University Press, Carlton, 1966

Pike, D., *Paradise of Dissent: South Australia 1829–1857*, Longmans, Green and Co., London, 1957

Richards, Eric and Herriman, A., 'Irish Women in Colonial SA', in *Irish Women in Colonial Australia*, ed. T. McClaughlin, Allen & Unwin, NSW, 1998

Richards, Eric, 'Irish Life and Progress in Colonial SA', *Irish Historical Studies*, vol. 27, no. 107, May 1991

Richards, Eric, ed., *Visible Women: Female Immigrants in Colonial Australia*, ANU, Canberra, 1995

Schmaal, E., *Clare, A Backward Glance: Stories of Early Clare and District*, drawings by John Haynes, Clare National Trust, c. 1980

Schmidt, B., *Mountain Upon the Plain: A History of Mount Barker and Its Surroundings*, District Council of Mount Barker, 1983

Smith, Russell, *1850: A Very Good Year in the Colony of South Australia*, Shakespeare Head Press, Sydney, 1973

South Australia, the Civic Record 1836–1986, Jubilee 150 Local Government Executive Committee, Wakefield Press, Netley, 1986

Steiner, Marie, 'Matthew Moorhouse: A Controversial Colonist', Historical Society of South Australia, no. 31, 2003

Steiner, Marie, 'Michael Ryan and the Female Immigration Board in South Australia', *Journal of the Australian Catholic Historical Society*, vol. 24, 2003

Stratton, J., ed., 'Biographical Index of South Australians 1836–85', South Australian Genealogy and Heraldry Society, Adelaide, 1986

Whitelock, Derek, *Gawler*, Corporation of the Town of Gawler, 1989

Willunga National Trust, *Willunga Walk*, nd

Willunga National Trust, *Willunga Courthouse and Police Station*, rev. edition, 1976

Willunga Progress Association, *Willunga: 'Place of Green Trees'*, Adelaide, nd

Withers, Ann, *Inside the Clare Valley*, Seaview Press, Adelaide, 1998

Wakefield Press is an independent publishing and distribution company based in Adelaide, South Australia.
We love good stories and publish beautiful books.
To see our full range of books, please visit our website at
www.wakefieldpress.com.au
where all titles are available for purchase.
To keep up with our latest releases, news and events, subscribe to our monthly newsletter.

Find us!

Facebook: www.facebook.com/wakefield.press
Twitter: www.twitter.com/wakefieldpress
Instagram: instagram.com/wakefieldpress

www.ingramcontent.com/pod-product-compliance
Ingram Content Group Australia Pty Ltd
76 Discovery Rd, Dandenong South VIC 3175, AU
AUHW021028241125
419940AU00003BA/14

9 781743 055786